"My voice is strong, powerful—a force to be reckoned with. It wants to tell a story that inspires change. It wants to transform my soul. As I let go of my beliefs, conditions, and fears, my voice wants to travel to new places, meet new people, and be open to opportunities and change. It wants to cause a revolution in me: kill the old self as the new self emerges. It trusts my instincts, feelings, and awareness. It wants to not doubt, judge, analyze, or examine—too exhausting! It wants to tell my soul's journey of creative expression, a love story that travelled across different lifetimes to present day to complete a path, a journey—a destiny. Forces are driving me and catapulting me into a new direction of expansiveness, openness, adventure, and fun. I no longer need to be afraid but choose to let go and find myself: being grounded in love and compassion for myself, honoring who I am, and not denying or fighting that calling. I can no longer stay where I am—be who I am. I'm restless to bare my soul and continue my journey into awesomeness."

LIFE STORMS
HURRICANE KATRINA

Surviving Life Storms
Through Thriving Life Scripts

One of the Most Devastating Natural Disasters
in the History of the United States.

JENNIFER GREMILLION

Life Storms: Hurricane Katrina...
Surviving Life Storms through Thriving Life Scripts

978-0-9966026-0-0 (paperback)
978-0-9966026-1-7 (eBook)

Library of Congress Control Number: 2015911782

Printed in the United States of America

Life Scripts, LLC
3500 N. Hullen Street
Metairie, LA 70002
LifeScriptsPublisher@gmail.com

DEDICATED SPIRITUALLY
TO PIERRE, GABRIEL, AND LUCAS

~ Amazing Teachers,

~ Amazing Healers,

~ Amazing Love,

~ Amazing Grace.

AND

DEDICATED PERSONALLY
TO ALL SURVIVORS
~ Anyone Who Weathered a Storm in Life

"People are like stained-glass windows. They sparkle and shine when the sun is out, but when the darkness sets in, their true beauty is revealed only if there is a light from within."
~ Elisabeth Kübler-Ross

Table of Contents

Acknowledgments

Thank you to my husband, Pierre Gremillion, for encouraging me not to hold back in my writing; believing in me when I didn't believe in myself; and for loving me when I didn't love myself.

Thank you to my two amazing sons, Gabriel and Lucas. When I wanted to throw my writings away, Gabriel said, "Your life would be a waste. And God doesn't waste lives." Lucas has appreciated my skill of writing. He points out the beauty, "My mom is a writer."

Thank you to my mom, Connie Ward, for reading everything I passed her way and becoming part of my collaborative team. Shh. She really is a secret writer.

Thank you to my dad, Ken Ward, for telling me, "You're such a strong woman. You just don't know it yet. In fact, you are the strongest one in the family." I know my value and worth now.

Thank you to my aunt, Jackie Viola, for her inspiration, endless encouragement, and kind support along my journey.

Thank you to my sister, Lauren Fostel, for challenging me as a sister does; for reading my scripts along the way; and for staying close behind the scenes even if she didn't understand me at times.

Thank you to Jayne Ankeney for her vitality and contagious enthusiasm. She shared, "Jen, you got this. You got this." Those words echo throughout my day. You can do this Jennifer!

Thank you to Wayne Larocque and a friendship that began at The Esalen Institute in Big Sur. He has generously encouraged me with immense, profound, and poignant wisdom. He pushed me to go onwards and upwards.

Thank you Cathy Montalbano for seeing the depth of my soul and pointing out that I've overcome many obstacles with strength and faith.

Thank you Miriam Aliberti for reading my evolving scripts and for dialoging with laughter and tears. You are a true friend with a gentle and pure heart!

Thank you Darlene Dicharry for the energy of sweetness, availability, and gracious wisdom. Your words have pierced my heart with lightness.

Thank you Danielle Boyle for being the daughter I never had; for picking up my writing with eagerness and willingness; and for appreciating my vulnerable and transparent blogs.

Thank you Shelley Rike for shifting stuck and stagnant energy with your amazing hands and your overflowing heart. My wounds have become my medicine!

Thank you Paige Huffman for loving me and this story. When she shares my story, people cry every time—Paige included. It's time. Right?! It's time.

Thank you Victoria Lopez for a sustained friendship since 1st grade. You have always been a prayer away... a phone call away.

Thank you Mary Richard for a dear friendship and for never letting me go. Your love and support to your family and friends, including myself, is sweetness to my soul.

Thank you to my manager, Alexia Melocchi, at Little Studio Films, for believing in me and my writings. She said, "Jennifer, there is talent and there is a calling. Your talent is writing, but you are moving into a spiritual calling." Thank you for helping me get over my fears and be seen.

Thank you Jeffrey Smith for teaching me how to love myself; for embracing my shadow, flaws, and imperfections; and for teaching me that I'm truly amazing.

Thank you Michael Berger for encouraging me on this path and equipping me with spiritual protection and spiritual empowerment.

Thank you for the visible support and the invisible support. Divine forces pushed me in this direction. It's been an amazing journey. I'm forever grateful for all the teachers, healers, and lovers, from experience to experience, teaching me every step of the way. *May you fathom the breadth, length, depth, and height of my sincere appreciation.*

Preface

We all go through storms in life or "Life Storms." We either crumble or courageously come out of it with a story to tell. A *Life Storm* is the precipitating event, the trigger that incites a reaction. Unfortunately, it is usually the same reaction–an ingrained pattern when the storms of life crush upon you. This book is the first in the series of *Life Storms*.

Originally, I wrote bits and pieces in a screenplay called **LIFE STORMS**, but readers wanted more details or they didn't believe these things happened.

I decided to write a book with additional details and unique perspective. Since these are my experiences and growth, I wanted to impact and encourage the reader to go on their own self-discovery process. I pose questions and points for reflection. This writing experience is called *Life Scripts*.

In psychological terms, *Life Scripts* are often described as the expectations and beliefs of others that form a script for us to live with and follow. Many people are actors and follow their prescribed script. Some don't question and don't change it. When we realize that we are living out a script that was written "for us" and not "by us," then we can begin writing our own *Life Script*.

I discarded my old script and wrote a new one. I edited, directed, and created my life with awareness. I became the master of my heart and soul and tossed out all other scripts. A *Life Script* with beauty, meaning, and understanding.

The goal is to move from Life Storms to Life Scripts to Life Success!

Each chapter of this book begins with a scene or sequence from the screenplay, **LIFE STORMS**.

LIFE STORMS is my true story—"A heartbroken mom blames herself for the birth of her son's rare disease and her resistant husband emotionally departs from their marriage as Hurricane Katrina wreaks havoc... unraveling another *Life Storm*."

When I share my family's story, the next question is "When are you going to write a book?" I only considered myself a screenwriter until I edited my own *Life Script*. Now,

I WRITE...

I write riveting screenplays.

I write inspirational blogs.

I write love letters.

I write needed encouragement.

I write imperative teacher's notes.

I write fun and sometimes required emails.

I write color-coded post-its and long to-do lists.

I write melodic birthday cards.

I write published poems.

I write esoteric observations.

BUT MOST OF ALL...

I write to learn, grow, and discover.

Who am I? Why am I here? What is my purpose?

I write from my heart and create from my soul. My strong, powerful voice resonates into memorable, multi-layered characters with thought-provoking concepts. I pursue dynamic and intriguing places within my persona and wrestle with the great yet sensitive challenges of the heart and soul. My deep and inspirational well flows from extraordinary and courageous experiences of life. My raw, transparent voice invokes profound change, deep conversation, soul searching, purpose, and inspiration.

Writing is my essence, passion, and promise to my vibrant soul and authentic self!

Life Storms: Hurricane Katrina is a love story to myself and others: untold stories, impetuous growth, gripping challenges, lessons learned, realized miracles, and the immense beauty of it all.

I grew up in New Orleans, Louisiana. And anyone that has visited knows there is a flair and a flavor to the New Orleans culture.

I was an Uptown girl. I lived on Sycamore Street and Henry Clay Avenue. I rode the St. Charles streetcar and ate at The Camellia Grill. Every Friday evening, our family ate at Petrossi's Seafood. My brother, Brent, ordered the same... grilled cheese.

My sister, Tania, and I took the Magazine bus to Canal Avenue. We ventured downtown and shopped at Woolworths Drugstore. I stocked up on candy at Uptown Square Shopping Center. Grabbed an ICEE™ at 7-Eleven. Delighted in Sunday outings at Plum Street Snowball. Another pink lemonade please.

We enjoyed Mardi Gras parades on St. Charles Avenue and Tchoupitoulas Street. The flambeaux carriers lit up the sky with heavy blazing torches. My enthusiastic mom jumped up and down and naturally the numerous beads followed.

I was literally a hop, skip, and jump away from my next school. You could cross the street from my grammar school to high school to college. I attended Holy Name of Jesus, Mercy Academy High School, and Loyola University. I completed a year at Loyola University Law School but immediately knew that was not for me. My father and grandfather were lawyers. And I was engaged to a lawyer. End of story.

Our house was the one that everyone gravitated toward and where all the action was: an open and revolving door of friends and family members. My mom was always cooking and cleaning. My dad was consistently blaring his stereo. My brother was constantly banging his drums.

But I also remembered the floods: part of life—part of living in an Uptown neighborhood. In fact, my siblings and I walked home from school in flood water. Cars couldn't drive down the streets. And if they did, they could possibly send waves of rising water into homes. We walked a mile and a half in flood water. But guess what? We didn't think anything of it. It's what we knew. It's what we did.

As I child, I remembered the heavy rains, floodwaters, and school closings. But as an adult, I remember and will always remember Hurricane Katrina.

Introduction

Life for me was a "fight or flight" — an emergency response — the red flag on the beach warning, "Don't enter the water." But I entered the raging waters.

A friend once told me, *"Jennifer, if we go to war, I want you by my side. You are a survivor."* A sincere comment, but did I recognize my strength and courage? Many times, I was tossed to and fro, not knowing how to make sense of things.

But am I a survivor?

I had to discover that truth for myself as I went into an internal world. Hard to keep my feet on the ground, I was inundated with inspiration and intuition at light speed. The energy was invigorating. The energy was exhausting. I needed spiritual protection and spiritual empowerment to digest, to process, to understand. All my internal work was coming to light. *No longer hidden in my shadow. No longer shackled with fear. No longer.*

I AM A SURVIVOR.

I survived being hit by a drunk driver.

I survived a rape.

I survived suicide attempts. Yes, there were two.

I survived an emergency C-section.

I survived my son being born with Giant Pigmented Nevus, a rare medical condition.

I survived doctors telling me he would not live past a year.

I survived heartache.

I survived being misunderstood.

I survived my cauldron of emotions.

I survived my sensitivities and sensibilities.

I survived the instability in my childhood.

I survived the instability in my marriage.

I survived losing my home and possessions.

I survived only $50 in my pocket.

I survived Hurricane Katrina.

I AM A SURVIVOR!

This story is written from a survivor's point of view: the ups and downs, the ebb and flow. I've weathered the storms of life. And I'm here to share the untold beauty of it all. Captivating and riveting.

My husband, Pierre, said "You act like you have it all together. Like you don't need anyone's help. *But your strength is your sensitivity!* It's what you don't allow others to see."

The space where I'm the most vulnerable is where I find solace buried in the depths of my sensitivity. Naked... my soul awakens.

CALLING ALL SOULFUL READERS...

My soul was tethered and shattered in pieces. It was time to integrate and become whole. I went inward, exploring and discovering who I was and who I was not.

As deep calls to deep, my soul awakened in the light of my imagination, fantasy, dreams, and unlimited and boundless energy. Here, I'm free and uninhibited to no longer hide but to truly smile, dance, cry, make love, engage in meaning and purpose, and to feel the feelings that rock my world. As I fully embrace all of who I am, I experience thrill, intoxication, amazement, elation, enrapture, pleasure, gratitude, tenderness, attraction, and inner peace. This freedom allows me to be fearless and daring—understood and accepted.

As I undressed the old beliefs that enslaved me, I walked naked across a field, emptying myself with my soul to bare... Vulnerable and naked I stood. God clothed me in unconditional love. It was always there waiting for me. Once I realized, welcomed, and accepted it, the unimaginable bursts forth—beautifully displayed. And there, I found rest.

I became speechless by how much God loves me. He is for me and delights in giving me good gifts. Spirit quiets my soul as He orchestrates what must come... my soul's journey, which leaves indelible marks of unfathomable grace and contemplative joy. As Spirit guides me, I'm broken and humble. His vast and unbounded love holds my heart.

He beckons me to come dance as He holds my hands and gently pulls me closer to Him. Surprised by my reaction, I cry. He comforts me and enlightens me that I don't trust myself because of the intensity of my feelings, wants, and desires that run deep in this sea of energy. He assures me that I can trust others as I trust Him. He pulls me forward to rest my feet on top of His feet. As He spins me around, I see my faces in childhood, adolescence, through adulthood. As the King's glory of gold and the yellow sunrays surround my face, He assures me... this is my time.

No longer do I need to be afraid. Here, I beam, shine and radiate in my gifts, compassion, and brilliance. As my effervescence comes forth, my true essence emerges.

The time to embrace is now. It's all around me. As I'm emptied, I truly find myself. It's the essence of who I am and what I have to give. Everything is within me, and I am more than enough.

Heart & Soul,
Jennifer

The Catalyst
Life Scripts One

FADE IN:

INT. TULANE HOSPITAL - EARLY MORNING

Spacious labor and delivery room with sterile walls.

Hospital monitor BEEPS.

PIERRE GREMILLION, tired, glasses, slender, speaks with a southern accent as he holds a hand.

>   PIERRE
>   You don't feel that?

JENNIFER GREMILLION, piercing big blue eyes, black hair, fair skin, appears calm as she lays in the hospital bed.

>   JENNIFER
>   Not since the epidural.

DOCTOR SHELBY, no makeup, scrubs, spunky, examines Jennifer and cautiously observes the fetal heart monitor.

BEEP. BEEP. BEEP.

>   DOCTOR SHELBY
>   Contractions are on top of one another.
>   (to PIERRE)
>   Put on your scrubs.

Pierre's face appears "alarmed."

>   DOCTOR SHELBY
>   (to JENNIFER)
>   Need to get the baby out immediately.

>   PIERRE
>   Is the baby --

DOCTOR SHELBY
Don't have a minute to waste. Losing
too much oxygen.

LABOR AND DELIVERY NURSE, young, overweight
with acne, pushes Jennifer's hospital bed…

TO THE OPERATING ROOM…

STAFF preps.

ANESTHESIOLOGIST, soft spoken, wrinkled face
appears over the green mask, sticks Jennifer's
legs with a needle.

ANESTHESIOLOGIST
Do you feel anything?

JENNIFER
No.

Needle gently pokes her.

ANESTHESIOLOGIST
This?!

Jennifer nods no.

ANESTHESIOLOGIST
(to DOCTOR SHELBY)
Clear.

Doctor Shelby cuts.

Pierre grabs Jennifer's hand. His face reflects
"trepidation."

PIERRE
I love you. You're in good hands.

Jennifer's face reveals "uncertainty."

                    JENNIFER
          Don't want to watch?!

                    PIERRE
          I've seen enough from my clients'
          medical records.

Anesthesiologist touches Jennifer's shoulder.

                    ANESTHESIOLOGIST
          Are you comfortable?

Jennifer's face reads: "I guess."

                    ANESTHESIOLOGIST
          Feel any pressure?

                    JENNIFER
          A slight pull and tug.

Anesthesiologist rubs her shoulder.

                    DOCTOR ASSISTANT (O.S.)
          What is it?

Doctor Shelby's tone is "angst."

                    DOCTOR SHELBY (O.S.)
          I don't… I need --

Pierre appears "vigilant."

                    DOCTOR SHELBY
                 (to PIERRE)
          Come here?

Jennifer grabs Pierre's arm.

                    JENNIFER
          What's going on?

                    PIERRE
          Hold on.

Pierre tensely approaches.

> DOCTOR SHELBY
> (to PIERRE)
> I've never seen anything like this.

GABRIEL GREMILLION, newborn, black and brown spots cover his body, whimpers. One giant spot covers his back, neck and scalp area. Over a hundred spots range from a dime size to a grapefruit size.

Pierre holds his chest and breaks down.

Jennifer grabs the anesthesiologist.

> JENNIFER
> What is it? Tell me.

> ANESTHESIOLOGIST
> (to JENNIFER)
> They have good doctors at Children's Hospital.

Chaos in the operating room.

> JENNIFER
> I want to see him.

Gabriel blubbers as they clean him.

> ANESTHESIOLOGIST
> You will.

Pierre paces slowly.

> DOCTOR SHELBY
> (to PIERRE)
> His Apgar scores are good.

OPERATING ROOM NURSE wraps Gabriel in a blanket and fixes his blue and pink striped hat.

                    OPERATING ROOM NURSE
          Daddy, would you like to hold your son?

She hands Gabriel to Pierre.

                    PIERRE
          I love you.

Pierre wipes his tears and kisses Gabriel.

                    PIERRE
          Daddy loves you. I'm here for you.

Jennifer notices the "anguish" on Pierre's face as he draws near.

                    PIERRE
                 (to JENNIFER)
          We'll get through this. Trust me.

Pierre places Gabriel on Jennifer's chest. Jennifer wells up with a mother's love.

                    PIERRE
          We have our faith Jennifer. Remember…
          And our love.

Jennifer remains steady.

                    JENNIFER
          Hi Gabriel. It's me, mommy.

Gabriel stares with soulful eyes and markings on his face and neck. Jennifer gazes tenderly.

                    JENNIFER
          You are beautiful. An angel with those
          cupid lips and almond shaped eyes.

She gently touches his face and smiles.

BRIGHT OVERHEAD SURGICAL LIGHTS DIM TO BLACK SCREEN.

HEARTBEAT SOUND.

> DOCTOR #1 (V.O.)
> It's called Giant Pigmented Nevus. An overconcentration of melanocytes.

> DOCTOR #2 (V.O.)
> A mutation of pigment cells in the 7th to 12th week of gestation.

> DOCTOR #1 (V.O.)
> No known cause. No known cure.

> DOCTOR #3 (V.O.)
> Don't know if he will live past a year.

> DOCTOR #2 (V.O.)
> Can be fatal… fatal… fatal.

HEARTBEAT FLATLINE.

FADE TO BLACK.

The Catalyst

Chapter 1
We'll Get Through This

Nevus is the medical term for birthmark. Melanocytes are pigment producing cells. Giant Pigmented Nevus can cover a significant portion of the body. The nevus can cover 85% of the skin surface.

Giant Pigmented Nevus is an overload of melanocytes that occurs during the 7th to 12th week of gestation. Approximately 1% of infants are born with a mole. However, Giant Pigmented Nevus occurs in 1 in 500,000 births. Neurocutaneous melanocytosis (nevus found on the brain and spinal cord) occurs in 1 in a million births.[1] Gabriel Gremillion was born with both.

The birthmarks can be black or brown in color and vary in texture from leathery to smooth. Since the birthmarks do not have as many sweat glands as normal skin, it is hard to stay cool.

Currently, there are 860 children and 375 adults with Giant Pigmented Nevus.

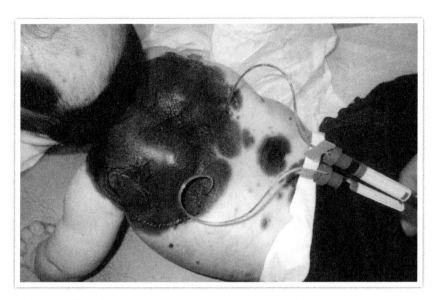

Gabriel's Giant Pigmented Nevus on his back. Draining tubes and stitches followed surgery.

It is not only a cosmetic issue; it can also be neurological. Some children have seizures, while others have hydrocephalus (a buildup of fluid in the cavities deep within the brain that puts pressure on the brain). They may require a shunt in their brain or spinal cord.

There is an increased risk of malignant melanoma (the deadliest form of skin cancer), leading to an increased risk of death. Sadly, some children do not make it.

Pierre Gremillion, my husband, went into action mode like a superhero. He attended each of Gabriel's surgeries in Chicago. He became heavily involved with the nonprofit Nevus Outreach, Inc. In fact, he volunteered as chairman of the board of directors from 2003 to 2010. We became involved in three fundraisers to benefit Nevus Outreach, Inc.

I was focused on the care of Gabriel: the next surgery, the next three-month tissue expansion period, keeping him healthy and comfortable, and keeping him inside, away from the sunlight. He itched nonstop due a lack of sebaceous glands.

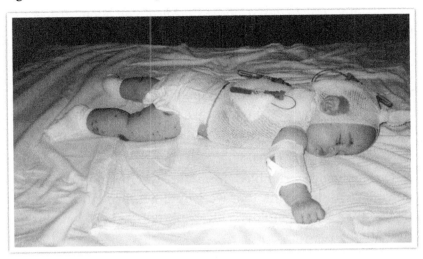

Gabriel after surgery with arm restraints, bandages, and draining tubes.

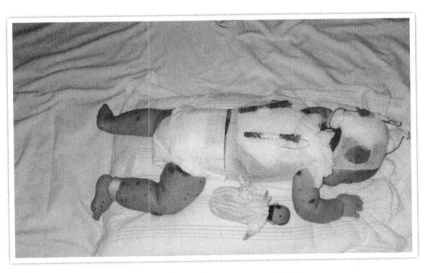

The nurse gave Gabriel a doll with his replicated nevus areas.

Moreover, there was an undercurrent in us personally and in our marriage.

I internalized. I was heartbroken and dealt with my internal struggle. My mind became my battlefield. And a battle was fought daily. *Did I cause Gabriel's medical condition? If there is no known cause, I acquiesced that it must be me.*

Pierre resisted. He became emotionally detached from me and emotionally connected to every need of Gabriel. He became despondent and overwhelmed, managing his own struggle, the surgeries, and his workload. Pierre is a lawyer and wanted to fight the condition like a courtroom battle.

Will our marriage survive?

Our marriage crumbled from the weight of the circumstances. We didn't think that we would get through it. We discussed divorce, unemployment, bankruptcy, and foreclosure along the way.

More importantly…

Will our child survive?

Will Gabriel live past a year?

We began a quest for doctors. As parents, we did everything we could do. We visited doctors in Sacramento, San Francisco, New Orleans, Slidell, and Chicago. We tried laser surgery, but it burnt a portion of Gabriel's skin. There was a chance nevus could reoccur after laser treatment, and it did. There was a chance that nevus could reoccur after surgery if the doctor didn't completely remove the adipose or fat tissue. After interviewing specialists, we decided on Dr. Bruce Bauer. He is a pediatric plastic surgeon who specializes in nevus removal at Children's Memorial Hospital in Chicago. Dr. Bauer surgically removed portions of Gabriel's Giant Pigmented Nevus.

Gabriel underwent one painful surgery after another. The tissue expansion process lasted three months. It involved inserting a tissue expander, or balloon, underneath his skin and filling the tissue expander with saline weekly or bi-weekly. The goal was to stretch his "good" skin and remove portions of his nevus. Instead of donor tissue grafts, tissue expansion allowed us to use Gabriel's own skin and provided better blood supply and tissue match. And of course, infections brewed, more antibiotics were needed, and ER visits were frequent.

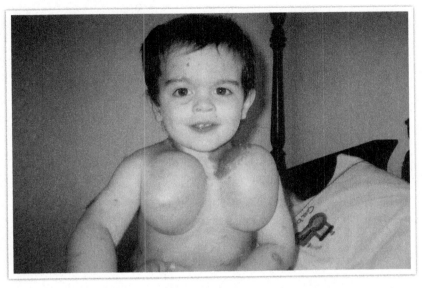

Tissue expanders placed in Gabriel's chest to create new skin.

Gabriel didn't swim or ride bikes. We filled his days with library visits, R.E.A.D. groups, outings to museums, and street-car rides. TV and games were introduced.

Gabriel was recovering.

And so were we.

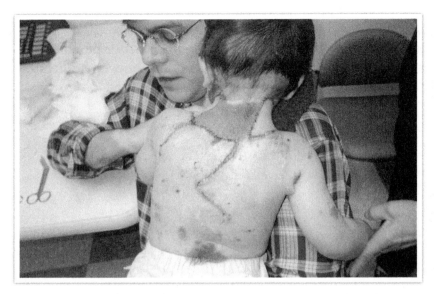

Tissue expanders removed from Gabriel's back. Skin was made and stretched. Numerous dissolvable stitches remained.

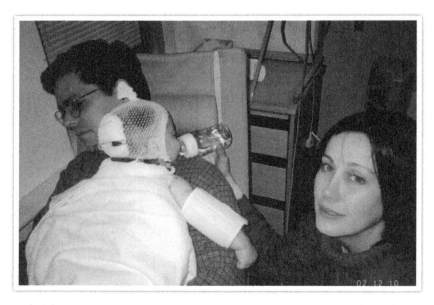

Gabriel was in post-op recovery with arm restraints and draining tubes. Jennifer fed Gabriel a bottle as Pierre held him.

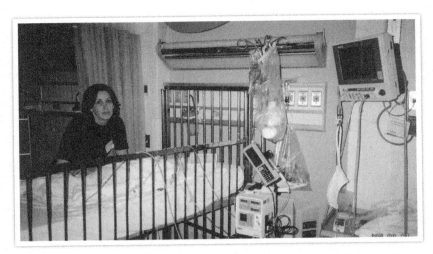

Gabriel recovered after surgery in the hospital crib as Jennifer stayed by his side.

Gabriel slept on Pierre's chest.

Gabriel was our focus at the time of Hurricane Katrina. He was three-years-old and underwent ten surgeries at Children's Memorial Hospital in Chicago. We needed to make it to number eleven, which was scheduled for November 1, 2005 – two months following Hurricane Katrina.

As I was facing this personal storm, there was another storm raging in the Gulf of Mexico.

The Catalyst

Chapter 2
When Disaster Strikes

What qualifies a natural disaster?

A disaster is a sudden, calamitous event that seriously disrupts the functioning of a community or society and causes human, material, and economic or environmental losses that exceed the community's or society's ability to cope using its own resources. Often caused by nature, disasters can have human origins too.[2]
(VULNERABILITY + HAZARD)/CAPACITY = DISASTER
What a combination!

A disaster occurs when a hazard impacts vulnerable people with the inability to reduce negative consequences.

We've seen on the news, read in the papers, or watched a documentary on the 2004 Indian Ocean tsunami, the 2010 massive earthquake in Haiti, the 2014 devastating fires in Chile.

Ten World Worst Disasters[3]...

1. The deadliest earthquake in July 5, 1201 in Egypt and Syria.
2. The Black Plague between 1347 to 1350 in North Africa.
3. The Indian famine in 1769.
4. The Irish Potato famine of 1845 to 1848.
5. The deadliest drought in China between 1876 to 1879.
6. The flu pandemic across the world from 1918 to 1919.
7. The Yangtze, Yellow, and Huai River Floods in China from July to August 1931.
8. The Chinese famine between 1959 to 1961.
9. The African drought in 1981 to 1984.
10. The North Korean famine and floods from 1995 to 1998.

I went way back. But they are reminders, no different than a memorial site—a remembrance of historical events—events people endured and courageously overcame.

What I surmise from natural disasters: *Change is certain. Disasters are inevitable. Fatalities cannot be escaped.*

Disaster happens on foreign soil and domestic soil *alike.* Disaster strikes all.

Ten U.S. Worst Disasters[4]...

1. The Great Chicago Fire of 1871.
2. The Johnstown flood in Pennsylvania in 1889.
3. Hurricane Galveston in 1900.
4. The Great San Francisco fire and earthquake in 1906.
5. The Tri-State Tornado in 1925.
6. Okeechobee Hurricane in 1928.
7. The Dust Bowl of the early 1930s.

8. The heat wave of the summer of 1980.

9. The heat wave of the summer of 1988.

10. *And Hurricane Katrina in 2005.*

Bingo! This is the one I wish to share with you: the aftermath, the renewal, the rebuilding on my life and my family's life following Hurricane Katrina—the vulnerabilities that follow another life storm.

A disaster occurs when a hazard impacts vulnerable people.

LIFE SCRIPTS
REWRITE, REDIRECT, RECREATE

» *How vulnerable are you?*

» *What determines your vulnerability?*

» *The part of you capable of being wounded or hurt.*

» *The sensitive exposure of it all.*

» *What storm in life did you face?*

» *What storm in life are you facing?*

HURRICANES

The Atlantic hurricane season officially runs from June 1st to November 30th. However, hurricanes have occurred outside of this period. The dates were selected to encompass over 97% of tropical activity. June 1st has been the traditional start of the Atlantic hurricane season for decades. However, the end date has slowly shifted from October 31st to November 15th to the current date of November 30th.[5]

There is an Atlantic basin peak season from August through October:

- 78% of the **tropical storm days,**

- 87% of the **minor hurricane days** (Category 1 & 2), and
- 96% of the **major hurricane days** (Categories 3, 4, & 5).

Maximum activity occurs early to mid-September. Tropical cyclones may occur out of season, primarily in May or December.

What do the categories mean? According to the Saffir-Simpson Hurricane Wind Scale...[6]

CATEGORY	WIND SPEED (MPH)	STORM SURGE (FEET)
5	156+	More than 18
4	131-155	13-18
3	111-130	9-12
2	96-110	6-8
1	74-95	4-5

During the past century, hurricanes have flooded New Orleans six times.

The New Orleans hurricane of 1915 was an intense Category 4 hurricane that made landfall near Grand Isle, Louisiana during the 1915 Atlantic hurricane season. It killed 275 people and caused $13 million in damage.[7]

The Louisiana hurricane of 1940 reached south of the Mississippi River Delta as a Category 2 with maximum sustained winds of 100 mph. The hurricane moved ashore near Sabine Pass, Texas at peak strength. It generated rough seas and strong storm surges of 6.4 feet. High tides flooded many of Louisiana's outlying islands. Rainfall made it the wettest tropical cyclone in state history. It was a slow-moving hurricane. Property, livestock and crop (corn, cotton, pecans) damage was due to the torrential rainfall in low-lying areas. Entire ecosystems were altered. The storm caused 7 fatalities and $10.75 million in damages.[8]

Major hurricane of 1947 affected the Mississippi Gulf Coast and the New Orleans region. This hurricane made landfall again as a Category 3 on the Mississippi and Louisiana coasts. A storm surge of 16 feet occurred in the Slidell area of Lake Pontchartrain. Most of downtown New Orleans was flooded extensively due to tidal surges from Lake Pontchartrain. Ninety-percent of the damage was caused by water. It was responsible for 51 deaths and more than $700 million in damage.[9]

Hurricane Betsy (1965) was a Category 3 hurricane when it made landfall in southern Florida, bringing storm tides of 6 to 10 feet. High winds, tidal flooding, and beach erosion caused substantial damage. Betsy continued across the Gulf of Mexico and approached the U.S. Gulf Coast. The storm surge pushed the Mississippi River into Lake Pontchartrain. New Orleans suffered its worst flooding since 1947. Betsy claimed 81 lives and inflicted $1.4 billion in damages. It was the first U.S. hurricane to ensue billion-dollar damage. *But it wouldn't be the last.*[10]

Hurricane Camille (1969) moved inland as a Category 5 hurricane just east of Bay St. Louis, Mississippi. It destroyed all the wind-recording instruments in the landfall area. An unprecedented storm surge of 25 feet crashed into the Mississippi Coast. The northerly winds pushed a massive surge of water through the marshes. Mississippi River levees were destroyed. Along the coasts of southeastern Louisiana, Mississippi, and Alabama, 5,238 homes were destroyed. The death count for the U.S. was listed at 256. Damages exceeded $1.4 billion.[11]

Hurricane Katrina (2005) downgraded from Category 5 to a Category 3 when it came ashore near Buras, Louisiana on August 29. *It was one of the most devastating natural disasters in* *the history of the United States.* Storm surge flooding was 24 to 28 feet along the Mississippi Gulf Coast. Storm surges west of the hurricane eye path, including New Orleans, were between 10 and 19 feet.[12]

The surge severely strained the levee system in the New Orleans area. Levees and floodwalls were breached and/or overtopped. Eighty-percent of the city of New Orleans was flooded up to 20 feet. The number of fatalities was estimated to be about 1,500 spread across four states with several hundred persons still reported missing. Katrina produced at least $108 billion in damage and is the costliest U.S. hurricane on record.[13]

Katrina was the most destructive and deadliest Atlantic hurricane for 2005. It was the deadliest U.S. hurricane since the **1928 Okeechobee hurricane** (where 1,836 people died in Florida, mainly due to a 6 to 8 foot lake surge; 312 people died in Puerto Rico; and 18 more were reported dead in the Bahamas. Total damage from the Okeechobee was estimated at $100 million).[14]

In 48 hours, Katrina reached maximum wind speeds of 172 mph. Katrina's peak strength was comparable to Hurricane Camille's intensity. However, Katrina was a larger storm and impacted a broader area of the Gulf Coast.

On Monday, August 29th, 2005, Hurricane Katrina made landfall in the greater New Orleans area as a Category 3 hurricane. Katrina brought 120 mph winds, 8-10 inches of rain, and a recorded tide increase of over 14 feet. The hurricane lost strength on its way inland, registering as a Category 1-2 storm. The devastation and loss of life made it one of the greatest natural disasters in the history of the United States.

Katrina was not the only hurricane in the 2005 season. There were other players.

Hurricane Wilma (2005) made landfall near Naples, Florida as a Category 3 hurricane. Storm surges ranged from 4 to 8 feet. Storm surges resulted in considerable flooding over portions of the Keys. Wilma caused the largest disruption to electrical service in Florida. The damage was estimated at $20.6 billion, and Wilma was responsible for 5 deaths.[15]

Hurricane Rita (2005) downgraded from a Category 5 to a Category 3 at landfall near Johnson's Bayou, Louisiana. Rita produced significant storm surges that devastated some coastal communities and flooded areas from Texas to the Florida Keys. Storm surges in the Cameron, Louisiana area were 15 feet high. A surge flooded the shores from Galveston Bay to the Florida Keys. Hurricane Rita was responsible for 7 deaths. Damages were estimated to be around $12 billion.[16]

Hurricane Ophelia (2005) brushed the Outer Banks of North Carolina as a Category 1. Ophelia caused storm surges of 4 to 6 feet above normal tide along the North Carolina coast. One death is associated with Ophelia. Damages were estimated at $70 million.[17]

Hurricane Dennis (2005) made landfall as a Category 3 on Santa Rosa Island, Florida with a storm surge of 6 to 7 feet extending inland over portions of the southeastern United States. Storm surges of 2 to 6 feet occurred in other parts of Florida, Alabama, Mississippi, and southeastern Louisiana.

Dennis was directly responsible for 3 deaths in the U.S. with damages estimated at $2.23 billion.[18]

September is national preparedness month. It's a reminder, and a great one, but truthfully, you prepare all year long. Hurricane season occurs from June 1st to November 30th. You have a six-month window of the possibility of hurricanes crashing in your town.

But many storms of life don't have a six-month window or an annual start and finish date. How do you prepare? Do you say "Hell with it" and ride it out? *How do you ride out the storms of life?*

The Catalyst

Chapter 3
Are You Prepared?

Preparedness occurs all year long. If you're not prepared, the storms of life can crush you.

I wasn't prepared when Gabriel was born. He was my first child. And like any new mom, I had to learn a new way of being.

I experienced so much pain and heartache in life. I wanted to know what it was like to be a mom enjoying this season:

Without the hurtful comments and stares...

Old lady bangs her wheelchair against my grocery cart. She squeals, "How dare you! Taking your son out so dirty. Too busy to bathe him. What kind of a mother are you?"

I added, "A helluva good one!"

Without the pain of leaving the house...

I went to buy diapers, and a neighbor approached me. "You should be arrested. Look at his bruises. I should call child protection services on you."

I came home and sat in a dark room. I held Gabriel. As he fell asleep in my arms, I wept.

Without my child crying throughout the night...

As a toddler, Gabriel repeatedly banged his fist against the ground. He shouted, "Why God? Why?"

He was in pain. Cysts would develop within his nevus. They would ooze, bleed, and bother him.

LIFE SCRIPTS
REWRITE, REDIRECT, RECREATE

» *Are you prepared for the storms in life?*

» *Emotionally? Psychologically?*

» *Mentally? Spiritually? Financially?*

» *When people attack, judge, and criticize you?*

» *What about when you criticize yourself?*

CAN YOU SURVIVE...

- Can you survive when your husband leaves you, not for another woman, but for another man?
- Can you survive when you discover your husband has a porn addiction and he is the pastor of a church?
- Can you survive the abnormal findings on your pap smear?
- Can you survive the same sex position for another twenty years?
- Can you survive your wife cheating with your best friend?
- Can you survive another night sleeping in separate rooms?

- Can you survive your friends suing you?
- Can you survive your family members gossiping about you? What about your dear friends?
- Can you survive when your credit card gets declined *again*?
- Can you survive running that red light?
- Can you survive the excruciating migraine when your kids are fighting?
- Can you survive the notice of default letters in the mail?
- Can you survive your aging parent's Alzheimer diagnosis and forgetting who you are?
- Can you survive the rise in gas prices?
- Can you survive another parent-teacher conference, only to hear the faults of your child?
- Can you survive no health insurance?
- Can you survive your son yelling that he hates your guts?

Can you survive?

Are you prepared?

Well-equipped and intentionally prepared for the ups and downs of life? Can you make it through another day without pills to get by? Can you make it through another day without the numbness of TV? Can you stand strong and authentically you without living someone else's life vicariously?

Life is full of detours, curve balls, dodge balls, and uncertainties. Most people are: barely surviving to make ends meet, struggling to raise kids, and wrestling with the deafening silence in their marriage.

Another day. Yes, another day.

I needed to be prepared: if Pierre and I got a divorce... if my son died... if our home was foreclosed... when our home was destroyed.

No one could turn my life around but me. I couldn't change anyone or anything. If I did, it became a measure of control. Yes, well-intentional but nonetheless control.

I wanted to be prepared *in season* when the storms prevail and *out of season* when the storms leave the harbor.

Prepared. It took me over forty years to get here. Attention stance. Ready? I am. Prepared? Fully.

HOW DID I PREPARE?

By going deep within the chambers of my heart and soul. *I needed to find my identity and stability.* I did internal work to create a new reality and to breathe new life. And lots of breathing I did. I discovered my own happiness and no longer relied on another person or another circumstance or another condition to dictate my happiness. No longer did I wobble, scatter, or toss to and fro. But I gathered and planted a heavy footing. I had to pull the weeds in my garden. I had to plant seeds in my garden.

These are some of the seeds that I planted...

I meditated. I practiced mindfulness. I saw a shaman. I embraced energy clearings. I invited pranayama into my practice. I ventured into esoteric science. I used essences, oils, and gemstones. I discovered the beauty of the chakra system. I invited an awareness on every level so I could handle another life storm *smoothly, graciously, and effortlessly.*

We entertain guests in our home, but we also entertain guests in our mind. What guests or thoughts did I allow in? Did I observe the host of my mind? I shifted my mindset... paid attention to what thoughts I allowed into my space. I paid attention to others' self-hate patterns. Was I taking on other people's energy? What was theirs needed to remain with them, not me. I had to ground and protect myself and call back my soul's energy.

I remain grounded, balanced, and whole: perfect in my imperfection—beautifully flawed to embrace my brilliance.

I became the observer. I gained control of my emotions. I chose to respond instead of react.

And I took no prisoners along. See, I was the prisoner: enslaved by false dichotomies; enslaved by self-limiting beliefs; and enslaved by beliefs from culture, church, school, family, government, medical community, and trauma. Old conditioning didn't resonate with my essence any longer. These beliefs needed to be shed—no different than when a snake sheds his skin... to embrace the newness. *I had to find Jennifer, not fix Jennifer.*

Since I can't fix anyone, including myself, I can only open up to the places and spaces within me to create healing and clarity—a trust that permeates every cell in my body—a knowingness that I am safe, secure, loved, and loving.

I set an intention for my life. Intention is all about energy: the desire, the drive, and the unharnessed momentum of pure energy. *A matter of the heart.* You intend an outcome and surrender to the universe. In contrast, goals are measurable. You analyze data and plan the necessary steps to reach an outcome by a certain date. *A matter of the mind. Matter of the heart versus matter of the mind.*

Independence weekend of 2013, I wrote my love note to the universe. This is my declaration. This is my intention of where I live. *This is a matter of my heart.*

"I'm on a healing journey, inviting clarity into my life; vibrating with love, peace, joy and bliss; renewing my awareness of passions, purpose, and patterns; trusting my intuition; attracting the people, situations, and opportunities needed into my life for my soul's evolution and my heart's expansion. Because something AMAZING is around the corner. It's so much bigger than me. Get ready to move forward!"

I surrendered and allowed the universe to enter my life in unbeknownst ways. It has allowed my heart to heal by changing patterns of thoughts and beliefs. Oh, how seamless it all can be, vibrating with unconditional love; not asking, demanding, or expecting, but finding the peace within myself; letting go of destructive patterns as light is shown in those dark areas; going into uncharted territories as I even write these words; inviting the encouragers, teachers, and guides into my life; being in a place of receiving instead of giving; learning to be content with who I am and where I am; attracting, magnetizing, and charging energy... filling me endlessly as I let go of a tight grip; and welcoming love in so many different ways.

It's my intention to reach my potential and dare to dream the impossible. This is the platform from which I now live.

LIFE SCRIPTS
REWRITE, REDIRECT, RECREATE

» *Have you set an intention for your life?*

» *Have you made a declaration to the universe?*

» *Are you ready to move forward? No longer content with where you are.*

» *Do you realize that something AMAZING is around the corner?*

» *When you sit quietly in the stillness, it will be revealed, knocking at your door.*

» *Will you answer the call to your soul?*

» *Will you write your intention for your life?*

» *It's a matter of the heart... your heart.*

» *Dig deep to unlock the pure energy... the amazing treasure.*

ON THE ROAD OF DISCOVERY

On my road of discovery, I learned many things about myself and my character.

- I love transparency.
- I love connection.
- I see solutions.
- I love to dance.
- I play music constantly.
- I love nature and walking my dog.
- I love the vastness of the ocean and the brilliance of a sunset.
- I love to lie in the grass and feel the nurturing vibrations of the earth.
- I love my boys' wisdom and insights. They have become my great teachers.
- I love my husband's patience.
- I love people's soul journeys. A place of returning to Source, Energy, Being, God.

No longer was I this little girl or young woman, unsure and unsettled, with the weight of other people's beliefs. I *am* a fearless and courageous woman that weathered many storms in life: the richness, the vastness, the depth, the intensity, and now the stability. I *am* safe, loving, loved, balanced, whole, creative, inspirational, strong, powerful, aware, and healed. I *am* a passionate and enthusiastic woman full of eagerness and willingness, loving and generous, giving and now finally receiving, practical and spiritual.

SPIRITUAL

At the age of 15, I penned these very questions...

Who am I? Why am I here? What is my purpose?

My sister, Lauren, once suggested, "We love when you decorate and organize, but we don't like when you are too spiritual."

Spiritual, huh?

What is spiritual? Aren't we all on a spiritual journey? Not a religious, moral, dogmatic or didactic journey, but one of healing and clarity?

A spiritual journey involves a return to my heart and my soul.

Return to inner peace.
Return to unconditional love.
Return to forgiveness.
Return to acceptance.
Return to compassion.
Return to understanding.
Return to joy.

These were the attributes I sought: *not* another gym or country club membership, *not* another pair of shoes or a sparkly diamond, *not* another car or house or vacation. These were attributes I was seeking! Attributes to engulf me instead of raging waters taking me down again or destroying another layer in my psyche. They were attributes beckoning me, knocking on my door, and calling me with the desire of embodying me.

I answered the call.

Will you answer the call? The call to your heart and soul.

We may not recognize it. Many times, we go through life on autopilot. I wanted my eyes wide open for this adventure called "my amazing life." I wanted to be filled with a fresh and heightened awareness, a beautiful awakening, eagerly alert to the treasures and wonderful gifts of the day.

Are you prepared?

Are you prepared for the storms of life?

Will you answer the call to your heart and soul?

Chapter 4
Should I Stay Or Should I Go?

On Saturday morning August 27, 2005, I awoke to do some computer work. Pierre kept close eye on the news. He said, "Jennifer, you need to come watch this." But my stubborn mindset was to finish my task at hand and furniture shop for Gabriel later in the day. He was graduating to a twin bed at the age of three. I thought, *"Oh another hurricane, it will pass."*

Hurricanes are part of New Orleans' culture. Many people do not understand why we live there. Why do we go through hurricane season each year? *It's what you know. Sometimes it's all you know. It's what you do.* There are strong and deep roots in New Orleans. You are born there, raised there, and most likely die there. There is a sense of belonging, a community where people know you and remember your name. You can't explain it. It must be experienced. And if you don't have that experience, you don't have a sense of knowing that this is where you belong.

Some matters of the heart cannot be explained. They must be experienced.

The Clash song, "Should I Stay or Should I Go," played in my head...

> *Should I stay or should I go now?*
> *Should I stay or should I go now?*
> *If I go there will be trouble*
> *And if I stay it will be double*
> *So come on and let me know*
>
> *This indecision's bugging me*

It's a decision to leave—a choice to make. If I go, there will be trouble: gridlock traffic, no gas, holding pee, hotel expenses, quarrels, and restlessness in the car. If I stay, there is a possibility of double: no electricity, no water, no food, hanging out in the attic, grabbing an ax to escape from the rooftop if the hurricane hits.

If you stay... You stock up on non-refrigerated groceries (in case you lose electricity), water, and batteries for your radio and flashlights. If you own a generator, all the power to you. Literally. In fact, many people bought generators after Hurricane Katrina.

If you go... You listen to local authorities on what route to take. They determine what threats can be expected and what necessary precautions need to be taken. Do we head to Florida? It could possibly hit there. Or do we head to Alabama? How about Arkansas? Can we stay close by in Baton Rouge? Can we visit relatives in Texas?

What do we take? Usually we pack an overnight bag. I have a clear container with wedding photos and baby books.

We board the house with wood over the windows and grey duct tape under the seams of the door. And we boogie out of there... to sit in traffic. Yes, roads are opened. Roads are closed. Contraflow is in effect.

Coastal areas, low-lying inland areas, and barrier islands are vulnerable to hurricanes and flooding. Since these areas have few evacuation routes, local officials ask people on barrier islands and in vulnerable coastal areas to evacuate immediately before the storm's landfall. We wait our turn.

You head to the gas station, maybe a few different ones because the lines are long or gas is not available at a particular station. Gas prices are not hiked up because it is a "state of emergency."

The tension builds as you listen to the radio.

Could this be the big one? Could this hit New Orleans? Could this change us?

And indeed Hurricane Katrina did!

From June 1 to November 30th, we must *make a decision* within a six-month period *if we should stay or if we should go.* It's not always easy. You watch and listen to the news, and assess the risks. Many people wait until they hear the words "mandatory evacuation."

The Catalyst

Chapter 5
What A Wonderful World

It was the last hurrah for us in New Orleans.

Gabriel, three-years-old, stood on stage with his class of performers. He was dressed in khakis and a white-collared shirt. He waved to his parents and grandparents. We waved back. Performers signed with expressive faces and big gestures to a song. Gabriel sung his heart out and swayed to the beat.

"What a Wonderful World" by Louis Armstrong played...

> *I see trees of green, red roses too*
> *I see them bloom for me and you*
>
> *And I think to myself*
> *What a wonderful world*
>
> *I see skies of blue and clouds of white*
> *The bright blessed day, the dark sacred night*
>
> *And I think to myself*
> *What a wonderful world*

Music Faded.

TV Played...

Weatherman stood in the rain as the waves of Lake Pontchartrain crashed in the background. Wind ripped. Sound muffled. Weatherman fiercely declared, "Once it hit the Gulf, the storm intensified from a Category 3 to a Category 5 in 9 hours. This will be catastrophic for parts of New Orleans and the metro area below sea level. *Possibility of an unprecedented cataclysm.*"

"Unprecedented cataclysm" echoed in my head... Gabriel's first MRI.

Pierre reluctantly entered the waiting room with wiped tears. He didn't need to say a word. His countenance spoke volumes. He ushered, "Jennifer, you need to hear this." Gabriel was five-weeks-old. I held Gabriel and walked down the hospital hall.

SILENCE.

Pierre opened the door to the radiology department. Three doctors stood, ready to disclose their findings. They delivered, "Gabriel has a lesion on his brain. It's on the left temporal lobe. Possibly nevus related due to his Giant Pigmented Nevus. We scheduled an appointment with Dr. Joseph Nadell, a neurosurgeon, to discuss options, possibly removal." I don't know how I made it out of the room.

"Unprecedented cataclysm" echoed in my head... Pierre frantically boarded the windows with a hammer and nail. He sealed the door crevices with duct tape.

The TV stated, "A mandatory evacuation of the city is in effect."

Gabriel rolled his Buzz Lightyear suitcase. Even though it was August and extremely hot, my red scarf dragged on the ground. Gabriel carried it since his first surgery—a part of me he won't let go of. It dragged as he entered the operating room. It dragged again on that day we departed.

Gabriel held my red scarf as he waited for another surgery.

I carried a clear container of photos. I packed it last year when we evacuated during Hurricane Ivan. Thankfully, I didn't empty it.

Pierre placed towels near the front door. He closed the door to our stucco home with French doors and gas lanterns. Pierre slammed the door to my green SUV. We drove down West Esplanade Avenue. I cautiously observed the boarded homes.

Gabriel clung to my red scarf. He was afraid and asked, "Are we going to be okay?" I assured him that we would and not to worry. I held his hand, remembering how many times I held him during surgery... during tissue expansion... during removal of stitches... during...

We are going to be okay. Lessons of life have taught me so much: Resilience, perseverance, and trust.

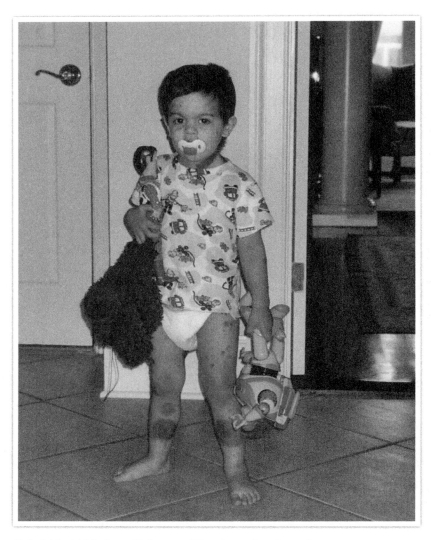

Gabriel held his Buzz Lightyear, Woody, and red scarf.

A survivor! Gabriel doesn't know it yet. Maybe he does. He is a survivor. We are survivors.

When you reflect on your life, may you gleam how many storms you have weathered. You've come so far. Release the tight grip and embrace your past, your present, and your future. You are a survivor. Shout it from the rooftops!

The Evacuation
Life Scripts Two

FADE IN:

EXT. GRANDMA MARY'S HOME - MORNING

1970's brick home. Green symmetrical hedge bushes.

GRANDMA MARY, eighties, stubborn, nervously sucks her teeth, locks the door.

>   GRANDMA MARY
>   Where's Gabriel?

Grandma Mary jerkily paces down the driveway.

>   JENNIFER
>   In my car. We need to hurry.

Jennifer grabs her grandma's luggage.

Grandma Mary opens her Chevrolet Impala door.

>   JENNIFER
>   Grandma, you can't drive your car.

>   PIERRE
>   We're inching in bumper to bumper
>   traffic.

ANNA, red fiery hair, wears a corrective boot, hangs onto Pierre and limps.

>   ANNA
>   Mom, listen.

>   GRANDMA MARY
>   (to ANNA)
>   Don't tell me what to do. I won't lose
>   my house and my car.

Grandma Mary slams her car door.

Pierre lowers Anna in the backseat.

                    ANNA
          Oww. Oww.

She rests her foot on a pillow.

Grandma Mary starts the ENGINE.

                    GRANDMA MARY
               (to PIERRE)
          Hurry up!

Pierre slams Anna's door shut and jumps in his
SUV.

                    PIERRE
          Your grandma is nuts!

Jennifer fastens her seat belt.

                    JENNIFER
          Stubborn as a mule.

CARS CRASH.

                    PIERRE
          What the hell?

Pierre and Jennifer frantically jump out.

Grandma Mary furiously points at Pierre as she
examines the crashed bumpers.

                    GRANDMA MARY
          Why didn't you back up?

                    PIERRE
          You didn't check your rearview mirror?!

Pierre observes the damage to the front of his
car.

She stomps.

GRANDMA MARY
Damn it! I'm ready to go.

JENNIFER
You need to ride with us.

GRANDMA MARY
Bull. I'm taking my car.

Gabriel rolls down the window.

Pierre throws his hands in the air.

PIERRE
(to JENNIFER)
Drive her damn car!

GABRIEL
I'll be okay mommy.

JENNIFER
What about --

PIERRE
Stay close behind me.

The Evacuation

Chapter 6
An Accident

A car accident was how we started the evacuation process. My grandma was a nervous wreck. *What if she lost her home? What if she lost her car?* It was too much for an elderly woman to process. She insisted on taking her car. And it was a good thing because her home was destroyed. It was the last day that she would live in that house... return to her home. *Did she know? Did she expect the worst?*

I drove my grandma's car as she sat in the passenger seat. Aunt Anna sat in the backseat with her foot propped on a pillow. She was recovering from bunion surgery. Pierre drove my SUV with Gabriel in his car seat.

Tension was thick. Tones were sharp. Communication was abrupt. Anxiety set in.

Car Radio Played...

1.2 million Residents of the Gulf Coast were under a mandatory and voluntary evacuation. Mayor Ray Nagin stated, "For residents who cannot leave the city, there will be shelters."

We headed I-10 East towards Baton Rouge. It took nine hours to get from New Orleans to Baton Rouge. Usually, the route takes one hour.

At the four-hour stretch, we passed a gas station with signage, "No Gas." Gabriel fidgeted in his car seat while Pierre drove. Finally, Pierre pulled in a parking lot. I jumped out my grandma's car and exclaimed, "My nerves are shot!"

Grandma yelled, "What are you two doing? I need to pee." Gabriel and Pierre peed on the side of a building. Grandma gasped, but truly it was the only solution. She shouted, "Pierre, better not look." As cars drove by, she peed. I peed. Aunt Anna wobbled out of the car humiliated, but realized this was the only solution. It was a time of crisis—a state of emergency.

We ventured back on the road. Grandma declared, "You can't seem to catch a break. You are about to lose your home. You have financial issues. Gabriel already had ten surgeries and needs more." I rubbed my neck nervously. Five more hours to go.

FINALLY BATON ROUGE

We arrived at my grandma's sister home. The home was already packed with other family members sleeping in every corner. There was no room for us.

She called her good friend and neighbor and asked, "Josie, can you take my sister and her group of four?" Green light— we headed to Josie's home. Josie opened the door with a sweet and warm face that embraced you as much as a hug embraced you. Josie insisted that Pierre, Gabriel, and I take her master bedroom. It was an arduous morning, an incredibly long day, and already a longer night. Everyone wanted to get to sleep— enough already.

There was a knock at the bedroom door.

My grandma entered the master bedroom in her tube socks, bra, and underwear. Astonished, I said, "You're not dressed! Pierre is here." Thankfully, Gabriel was asleep. But she injected, "I don't care! I just want you to know. Josie is dying! She has cancer. And she gave you her bedroom. Isn't that nice?"

Nice was an understatement. The whole situation was surreal. It was a blur. But nice? "Grandma, get to bed," I ushered.

The wind howled in the night sky.

I awoke the next morning to pitch black. I held Gabriel closely as we navigated the dark terrain. The house was lit with candles like a Catholic mass. I found Josie in the kitchen. She served us orange juice and cinnamon buns.

I found Pierre in the car... listening to the radio... listening to the effects of Hurricane Katrina.

Car Radio Played...

At 6:10 a.m., Hurricane Katrina made landfall on August 29, 2005 at Grand Isle, Louisiana as a Category 3 Hurricane with sustained winds of 140 mph.[19]

Power was out in Baton Rouge. Trees were down. Pierre looked at me, "We're heading to Texas. It's going to be a long one."

We evacuated to family members' homes in metro Houston and suburban Houston. We watched the news continuously, wishing it would end.

TV Played...

Images of a boat rested on a damaged home. A couple rescued from their rooftop. Louisiana Superdome damaged and surrounded by floodwaters. A man carried his daughter on his back through the floodwaters. Prisoners from Orleans Parish Prison staged on the highway.

My grandma set her hair with pink foam curlers and wore her yellow striped housecoat.

We watched looters take shoes and electronics. We sat in judgment. The nerve of them. But what if that was me? What if I was stuck there? Would I do the same? Maybe not the electronics because we didn't have power. What about medicine for Gabriel? Food for us? It's a thought to ponder before our critical and self-righteous mind sets in.

Dignity must be recognized in another human. You are worthy because of *who* you are and not *what* you do.

FLASHBACK: MY SLEEPOVER AT A FRIEND'S HOME.

I was burning up with fever at the age of eight. I was embarrassed because I didn't want to inconvenience anyone. But my friend's mom handled the situation with *grace and compassion.* She sat next to me on the bed and sang. She rubbed Vick's® VapoRub™ on my chest and turned on a humidifier. *She cared for me. She maintained my dignity.*

I recalled the memory in an instant. The flashback occurred. It was a gentle whisper… a gentle reminder of the grace and compassion that I was shown. Now, I was sharing the same grace and compassion.

A few years later, my friend's mom died of leukemia. But her legacy lives in my heart: teaching me when I was a young child—teaching me when I thought I wasn't aware. But *aware* I was. Impressionable. Dignity maintained.

All those moments… all these moments are preparation— seeds planted in your garden. Then, the opportunity presents itself. And you get to see those *seeds of grace and compassion flourish and bloom into the magnificence of dignity… of saving face.*

LIFE SCRIPTS
REWRITE, REDIRECT, RECREATE

» *When was the last time you saved face?*

» *When was the last time you maintained someone's dignity?*

» *People's hardships, pain, and suffering are expressed as beautiful manifestations of grace and compassion.*

» *We have all been there.*

» *Have you noticed?*

» *Are you aware?*

We really are all the same. May you recognize another's worth based on *who* they are and not *what* they do.

FLASHFORWARD: BACK IN TEXAS.

Everyone had their own set of difficulties and struggles. One sister-in-law was concerned about school and where her boys would attend now. The other sister-in-law was concerned about another Costco™ run as she made meals for twelve of us each day.

Everyone was thankful for a shower, a place to lay their head, and a meal to eat.

We moved 13 times in 5 weeks. Gabriel had an upcoming surgery on November 1st. We wanted to stay the course and stick to the plan.

But was there a plan? Really what plan did we have? Restlessness set in. Days turned into nights. Images flashed, and the news played like a bad song stuck in your head.

The Evacuation

Chapter 7
The Plan

There were postings on our church website, Lakeview Christian Center. Everyone was accounted for. But where would everyone go? People posted jobs in Little Rock, Arkansas, housing in Destin, Florida, a room in a house in Lafayette, Louisiana, a job in Beaumont, Texas.

But something came up... three apartments available in San Diego, California. I perked up.

We always wanted to move to California. Pierre applied to Pepperdine University in Malibu, California. I applied to Pepperdine University too. Neither of us got in. We were thinking the same thoughts in some distant place. But our paths didn't cross yet.

Over the years, Pierre and I looked at apartments in Santa Monica. Pierre pursued job opportunities in Los Angeles. He took the California Bar Exam. Our vacations were frequent in California. Family members lived in Redondo Beach, Monterey, and San Jose.

An apartment in California for a year. Is this the plan? Could this be a place to breathe again? A place to renew, refresh? A place to call home?

Pierre didn't think much about it. He had too much on his mind. He went out of town to Washington D.C. for an International Pigment Cell Conference. The conference occurred every three years, and Pierre didn't want to miss it. What if something incredible panned on the horizon for Giant Pigmented Nevus?

I stayed back and watched my mother-in-law sink into a major depression. She lost her business, and the roof blew off her home in her suburban neighborhood. It was the only destroyed home on her block. I took care of my aunt as she hopped around the house.

While in Houston, my sister wanted to buy me new clothes as the weeks went by. For some reason, I wasn't ready to take the plunge. I wanted to get back home and see what could be salvaged. Call it hopeful or call it denial. I just wasn't ready.

TV Played...

Levees breached or overtopped.

An image of our home surrounded by water.

The phone rang. "Did you see? Did you see the news? That was your house!"

Even though the hurricane hit, there was some notion of hope you hold onto. Maybe, our home made it. But once the levees broke, all bets were off.

Pierre returned from the medical conference. Reality set in. *Where will we live? Where will we go?* Overwhelmed, he inquisitively suggested, "Tell me about those apartments in San Diego." A week had gone by. I didn't know if they would still be available.

Hurricane Rita approached. Preparation plans were in order. Nerves were shot. My sister had windows all over her home. She was concerned that they could break from the wind damage. My grandma suggested that she could sit on top of the washer or dryer if floodwaters came in the house.

Your mind races with possibilities. Races for solutions. Races in the midst of uncertainty.

LIFE SCRIPTS
REWRITE, REDIRECT, RECREATE

» *Has your mind raced?*
» *Has it been in the depths of despair?*
» *Have you endured suffering?*
» *Do you know what it's like to go left or go right, to stay or run, to hide and cry?*
» *We have all been there at one point in our life. We are all the same. We are one!*
» *Where will you survive?*
» *What is the best place to keep you safe and secure... protected and assured?*

PRESS ENTER

We went from my sister's home to Pierre's sister home, back and forth in Texas, giving family members a break if that was even possible. I was fidgeting, antsy, and restless. And the glass of red wine didn't solve it—not even the bottle. A piece of chocolate cake didn't solve it—not even the whole cake.

My grandma sucked her teeth constantly. Pierre couldn't handle it anymore: the negativity, the news, the reality, the constant in the storm.

Pierre said, "I think we should go for it. Those apartments in San Diego. Gabriel can recover there. I can figure out this Hurricane Katrina mess. I need a place to work in peace." I did the happy dance in my head. *Finally, you came aboard.* The plan was shown through an email on our church website. "Three apartments in San Diego... free for a year."

Eagerly, I approached the computer and responded to the offer. My concerns were "safe and clean." I wanted to know that I was safe; no surprises, safe in my body, safe in my head, safe in my physical location. And it had to be clean; Gabriel had an upcoming surgery. Another tissue expander was to be inserted. There would be three months of filling the tissue expanders with saline weekly or bi-weekly. Oh, how I wanted a clean and pure heart to love, to possess inner peace, to experience joy again. Clean. Safe. Me. Us. How about you?

I typed away. Pierre and I said, "God's will be done." I pressed "enter." Lights flickered. The power went out.

PHONE RINGS

Five minutes later, the phone rang. Pierre noticed California on his caller id. He picked up his cell. Thank God for cell service. A big shout out for cell towers! Communication continued.

Steve Huffman was on the other line. Pierre seemed surprised. Steve continued, "I received your email. I didn't think anyone would want the apartments. No one has responded in over a week. Would you guys like to move to Encinitas, California?"

The conversation continued between Steve and Pierre. Fifteen minutes later, the power came back on.

Pierre mentioned the name of the apartments. I searched Google for "Poinsettia Ridge Apartments in Encinitas, California." I enthusiastically nodded, "Yes, this will work."

See, Steve was *paying attention*. He watched the Hurricane Katrina news event, and something tugged at his heart. Something said, "You can help in this situation."

LIFE SCRIPTS
REWRITE, REDIRECT, RECREATE

- » *How often do you get that tug... that nod... that reminder but you blow it off?*
- » *Or you don't have time or someone else can do it?*
- » *But those perfect moments are calling you...*
- » *Into something more, something deeper,*
- » *Something your heart and your soul yearns for.*
- » *Those perfect opportunities are your internal guidance system...*
- » *Prompting you, nudging you, guiding you.*
- » *You can do this. I purposed this in you.*
- » *You are capable.*
- » *You are powerful.*
- » *You are supported.*
- » *Just say yes. Just go.*
- » *Just open your heart for expansion and expression.*
- » *Will you answer the call?*

The Evacuation

Chapter 8
Return To New Orleans

Yes, another hurricane. And what an Atlantic hurricane season 2005 was!

Hurricane Rita downgraded from a Category 5 to a Category 3 at landfall near Johnson's Bayou, Louisiana. Rita produced significant storm surges that devastated some coastal communities and flooded areas from Texas to the Florida Keys. Storm surges in the Cameron, Louisiana area were 15 feet high. A surge flooded the shores from Galveston Bay to the Florida Keys. Hurricane Rita was responsible for 7 deaths. Damages were estimated around $12 billion.[20]

Three days after Hurricane Rita hit, we left Texas at night. Pierre cautiously drove on the I-10 Highway. High beams revealed dangling down power lines. Sparks flew. A pole fell on the highway. Pierre shouted, "Shit!" as he swerved off the road. Brakes screeched to a halt. I braced myself. Grandma sucked her teeth. Pierre yelled, "For the love of God, can you stop sucking your teeth!?" Anna rubbed her mother's arm.

Pierre proceeded, "This is stressful enough." A live electrical wire snaked around the road. Pierre drove. There was a repetitive thudding noise, and I curiously commented, "Pierre!" He pounded the steering wheel and forced, "Great!" Pierre pulled to the side: a flat tire. Furiously, he motioned, "Take everything out." Grandma instigated, "I should've drove my car back." Pierre flashed her a disdained look. Pierre implied, "You know how to change a flat tire." He slammed the car door. It was pitch black on the side of the road at 1:00 a.m.

SAVING HER LIFE

My grandma credited me for saving her life. What a big statement... to save someone's life. *Have you saved someone's life? Maybe, you saved someone's dignity without them knowing.* But she wanted me to know that there is no way she could have climbed up the attic ladder in her home and made it to the rooftop. She's not that strong. And my aunt was recovering from foot surgery. Neither of them had the strength. But I was prompted that evacuation day to go get my grandma and aunt. I could have evacuated with Pierre and Gabriel. My grandma and aunt would not have evacuated on their own. But things were orchestrated behind the scenes. Yes, there was temporary aggravation and frustration, but it was all part of a grand plan. I saved her life. I saved my aunt's life. I came for them.

When has someone come for you? People come all the time in unexpected ways in our journey. Do you notice them? The stranger that smiles, the neighbor who makes a meal when your son comes home for the hospital, the chatty person on the airplane speaking words of encouragement when you want to take a nap, a lover who won't let you go even though you've been terrible to them, the person who sees your talents and gifts when you don't see them, or the healers who want to remove your fear and shame. But only you can do the work. Yes, it involves work to come for someone, to invest in someone, to get your hands dirty. I've pushed people away. I've run. I've hidden. I've destroyed. I've taken what wasn't mine.

But in that instant, I came for her. Words resonated. Actions spoke volumes. It was a heart in motion. My heart spoke to her heart, my soul spoke to her soul, and we united in a tragedy— *one of the most devastating natural disasters in the history of the United States.* But it was more than a tragedy. It was a preparation. It was a uniting. It was a healing.

My grandma passed away nine years later. My mom and Aunt asked family members who would like to do her eulogy. My sister volunteered me. I thought to myself, "That's not me. She should do it." But in an instant, I heard the faintest whispers. "I've already prepared you. I've united you. I've healed you." And so I came for her once again.

REMEMBERING MY GRANDMA

Mary Braniff Viola, or Grandma Viola to me, was moved from nursing homes to hospitals seventeen times in her last year. On my last visit, I rubbed her arm and looked her in the eye. I said, "You've been a good grandma." Not believing me, she responded, "What have I ever done for you?" I honestly replied, "You were always there for me." Surprised but comforted, her face softened.

A month later, God's finger touched her as she breathed her last breath with a smile on her face. See, God showed His mercy as she received and accepted the love of Jesus. Her hurt and pain vanished in an instant as she entered His kingdom.

Her *presence* is how I want to remember her!

Mary was a special and unique woman: charming, beautiful, outspoken, strong-willed, determined, and very organized. She was a hard worker and even supported her parents when she was younger.

Some of her titles were accountant, bartender, and, at one point, a bookie. But the memorable titles were wife, mother, sister, aunt, friend, grandmother, and great-grandmother.

There are many lessons that she taught us.

The First Lesson is... *"Family sticks together no matter what!"*

When my grandpa became ill, it was challenging for all of us. Jack was so full of life, always joking and smiling. But it was more challenging for Mary as she cared for him through difficult times. She never stopped loving Jack, even if she had a funny way of expressing it.

The Second Lesson is... *"Help the one in need."*

Mary was beyond generous and put herself last for others consistently.

She valued relationships and other things, such as...

FOOD, GLORIOUS FOOD

Mary would never let anyone go hungry; she prepared delicious roast beef and gorgeous ham. Her pantry was always stocked with snacks, as friends and family members made frequent visits.

LOVE OF LEARNING

Mary fueled your body with food, but she also fueled your soul with her discovery quest. She studied the stars and cosmos, astrology, biorhythms, and color therapy to better understand our spiritual makeup, which made for many interesting discussions.

ADVENTURE OF TRAVEL

She loved to travel. Her spirit ventured to New York Broadway plays, danced at Carnival Balls in Washington with her husband, discovered the beauty of the Sistine Chapel in Rome with her daughters, delighted in the depth of Israel with her sisters, and was fascinated with the Great Pyramids in Egypt.

JOY OF STORYTELLING

Mary was entertaining. She enthusiastically referred to herself as "Grandma Viola" to everyone. She clipped coupons and snuck soda, sandwiches, and candy into the movie theater.

CAPTIVATED BY MOVIES

She was captivated by movies and had an extensive collection of VHS tapes, from *Gone with the Wind* to *Cleopatra*.

But her true love was...

FONDNESS OF FAMILY

On one hospital stay, we were told that she wouldn't survive. But her tenacious, fighting spirit proved otherwise. She awoke with tenderness in her touch, compassion in her eyes, and kindness in her voice. She asked, "Do you see those two angels there?" My mom, Connie, looked around. Anna replied, "Mother, who are you referring to?" She responded, "The angels are you two... my daughters."

I experience the love of family in Anna as she cared for her mom since Hurricane Katrina. Anna made daily visits to the nursing homes, gave insulin shots, and cooked meals.

I witness the love of family in Connie as she drove Mary to doctor appointments, picked up her prescriptions, and visited her in the hospital.

Connie and Anna are her two angels that breathed light, truth, and love into her.

Albert Einstein once said, *"Our death is not an end if we can live in our children and the younger generation. For they are us, our bodies are wilted leaves on the tree of life."*

Her Presence is Her Love.

Her presence lives in each of us... through the adventure of travel, reading, learning, studying, movies, and family.

My grandma has taken us on a journey... *healing in daring, uncharted territories to embrace the divine presence.*

"My soul is full of whispered song. My blindness is my sight. The shadows that I feared so long are all alive with light." ~ Alice Cary

May we go forth in light and hold onto the liveliness of cherished memories of Mary Braniff Viola. May we partake of the winsome voice of spirit; the sparkling light of truth; and the everlasting of unconditional love. Behold, God makes all things new!

Mary Braniff Viola enjoyed a cold beer in Monaco.

The Evacuation

Chapter 9
The Next Morning

After Pierre fixed the flat tire, we finished the drive from Houston, Texas to Mandeville, Louisiana. The Northshore, located north of Lake Pontchartrain in St. Tammany Parish, had a lot of tree damage and lost power.

Thankfully, my parents' subdivision, Beau Chêne, fared well. My parents didn't lose electricity. They were out of town when Hurricane Katrina hit, and they remained out of town for the four weeks following. Airports were shut down.

My sister, Tania, lived a few blocks away from my parents. Tania checked on my parents' home beforehand and gave us the green light to come back to Louisiana.

We arrived truly exhausted, and we passed out. It had been a whirlwind… literally.

The next morning, we drove to Tania's home. She bought a generator to make it through the power outage. If you didn't own a generator before Katrina, you sure well purchased one after Katrina.

Her TV played with the same devastation. I thought the Northshore would be different. They didn't get the damage like areas in New Orleans and the Gulf Coast. But it was the same crisis: the same state of emergency—the same—unsettling.

New Orleans was shut down. No one was allowed in the city unless they had a pass. Pierre had a pass since he was a business owner. Could we get in? Did we want to get in?

We couldn't sit around any longer. The suspense killed us. But the suspense of what? We already knew. We'd already seen our home on the news. *Still, we wanted to go home.*

We ventured to a po'boy shop and saw the look of hopelessness—the despair on people's faces. The strong became weak, despondent, displaced. You could see the damage had been done. Yes, the damage had been done.

Tania asked, "Are you sure you want to see your home?" I emphatically answered, "Yes."

Immediately, my mind flashed back to Gabriel's birth...

When Gabriel was born via emergency C-section, I held him on my chest for those few minutes. But, he was swiftly carried away by nurses and doctors.

Everyone was concerned about me. As I laid in the hospital bed recovering from the emergency C-section, I looked upward to numerous faces staring at me.

Hours went by. Everyone had seen Gabriel. But what about me?

Tania asked once again, "Are you sure you want to do this?" Sure was an understatement. Determined, resilient, prepared—I was ready to see my child. Once again, I emphatically answered, "Yes."

Finally, they brought Gabriel to me. I asked Pierre to unwrap the swaddling blanket. And I saw... the extent of his Giant Pigmented Nevus. And I came undone. I questioned silently and angrily, "Why God? Why?" Family members wept with me: my dad, my mom, my sister, my husband. They hugged me and encouraged me.

Will Gabriel survive? Will he live past a year? What did I do wrong? Blame, guilt, and fear set in.

Pierre had always been the rock. But I noticed his countenance change as the storms of life crushed upon him.

And as I looked at the faces in the po'boy shop, I saw faces change as the storms of life crushed upon them. I knew that face. I remembered that face. I knew that pain. I felt their pain.

How fragile we are.

"Fragile" by Sting played.

> *On and on the rain will fall*
> *Like tears from a star like tears from a star*
> *On and on the rain will say*
> *How fragile we are how fragile we are*
> *How fragile we are how fragile we are*

The Evacuation

Chapter 10
Evacuation Snapshots

Our friend, Johnny, lived in our neighborhood. When he called his insurance company to open a Hurricane Katrina home damage claim, the insurance company didn't believe him. Now, the levee broke within a mile radius from our home. The satellite photos revealed that houses were flooded. Roof damage was evident from the wind storms, but they didn't believe him.

Johnny was quick-witted. He drove from Houston to New Orleans. The Lakeview area was submerged with floodwaters. He found a canoe resting in a tree. He grabbed the canoe and proceeded into the Lakeview area. He took pictures of our church, Lakeview Christian Center. He paddled to our home and took pictures of our home for insurance purposes. He made it to his home and a friend's home.

TO HAVE OR NOT TO HAVE

After the hurricane, many people commented, "You had insurance. So, what is the big deal?" Insurance replaces your loss of monetary value. But it cannot replace the loss from destruction and devastation: emotionally, mentally, and psychologically. Anxiety, insomnia, destroyed lives, broken marriages, loss of life, suicides, uproot, and uproar. It cannot rebuild your life internally. *Only you can put a shattered heart back together... moment by moment... challenge by challenge... opportunity by opportunity.*

Isn't that what we really yearn for? A place of comfort? A place of safety? A quiet inner peace in the midst of the storm? Knowing everything is going to be all right? Knowing you will get through it victoriously?

You are powerful. You are capable. You are balanced. You are whole.

"When you live your life with an appreciation of coincidences and their meanings, you connect with the underlying field of possibilities." ~ Deepak Chopra

I desire to tap and tune into the underlying field of possibilities. Do you?

Was it a coincidence that a canoe was sitting in a tree for Johnny? He couldn't have navigated the floodwaters without it. The universe knew and supplied his need. Help was present. Solutions were available. Thank you for the underlying field of possibilities!

DROPPED WITHOUT NOTICE

When Gabriel was born, our health insurance dropped us: no notice, no phone call, no letter.

Pierre drove to Baton Rouge to show them pictures of Gabriel. This wasn't a cosmetic issue. This was a medical issue. Thankfully, Pierre is a lawyer, so he has the skill set to get the job done. And our health insurance was immediately reinstated. Gabriel was covered again. We were covered again.

But how many people have been denied a medical claim when they have insurance? Isn't that what insurance is for? To insure you? I think about the movie, *The Rainmaker*. Matt Damon was an idealistic attorney who took on a corrupt insurance firm with his cynical partner, Danny DeVito. Have you taken on an insurance firm? Have you taken on someone corrupt?

How many people fought their medical insurance claim? The insurance company hopes you give up—no different than a lawyer burying the opponent in discovery, interrogatories, and depositions.

How many people fought their homeowner's policy?

How many people eventually gave up?

How many people fought the good fight and won?

It's during those times when life becomes a mirror—a reflection. Everyone projects their own inner reality into an outer reality. You create your reality. If your inner reality is calm, balanced, relaxed, and grounded, then the outer reality can be in sync—congruent with who you really are. When those unpredictable and uncertain storms of life engulf you, they won't consume you. In fact, you can stand strong in the midst of the raging waters with your feet planted firmly on the ground. You can stand strong in your identity and stability. You can be dropped without notice but carried with grace and dignity—effortlessly, exponentially, and effectively because you know who you are and who you are not. You go deeper to discover an inner strength, unlimited resources, and beautiful capabilities. You don't get knocked down to dust yourself back up again. You stand firm with confidence and power—worth and value. Oh, how you are gloriously worthy in every way.

LIFE SCRIPTS
REWRITE, REDIRECT, RECREATE

» *Have you ever been dropped without notice?*

» *Dropped in a relationship without a phone call? Not even a text?*

» *Dropped from a job that you had for over 40 years?*

» *Dropped because the younger generation was moving on your turf?*

» *Dropped from a friendship...*

» *When you didn't understand what really went wrong?*

» *Dropped by other family members because their greed for an inheritance became their priority rather than relationships?*

» *Dropped from a school because the principal and staff didn't want to do their jobs?*

» *Dropped without notice?*

Coming Home
Life Scripts Three

FADE IN:

EXT. PIERRE AND JENNIFER'S HOME - DAY

SUPER: "SEPTEMBER 29, 2005. NEW ORLEANS, LOUISIANA."

NATIONAL GUARD on foot. Helicopters roar overhead.

Jennifer and Pierre in white hazmat suits and boots.

Pierre approaches the front door of his home.

Jennifer beholds her devastated neighborhood, destroyed home, and damaged car from the sidewalk.

OLDER MAN, plump, tender voice, grey-haired, jovial red checks, appears from nowhere and approaches Jennifer.

> OLDER MAN
> Some of your roof blew off too.

Jennifer sighs.

> JENNIFER
> It did.

Pierre shakes the front door.

> PIERRE
> Damn it!

Older man observes Pierre.

> OLDER MAN
> Sure you want to see the inside?!

> JENNIFER
> If my husband can get in.

Older man reveals an "understanding" face. He wipes the sweat from his forehead.

ON OLDER MAN...

He approaches Pierre.

Jennifer watches the man unscrew the hinge and break the door.

Older man motions "wait" to Pierre. Older man enters the home and proceeds to open the windows.

Pierre waits near Jennifer with a "distressed" look.

ON RED CROSS TRUCK...

BELL RINGS.

Distraught NEIGHBORS gather.

Surreal moment as Pierre hands Jennifer a meal. She holds the box reluctantly.

ON OLDER MAN, PIERRE, AND JENNIFER...

Older man reappears with muddy feet, dirty pants, wringing wet. He wipes the sweat with a handkerchief.

>   PIERRE
>   How does it --

Older man lowers his head.

Jennifer holds her mask.

>   OLDER MAN
>   You will need that.

Pierre shakes his head.

> PIERRE
> Thank you.

Older man gently rests his hand on Pierre's shoulder.

> OLDER MAN
> That's what folks do.
> (to JENNIFER)
> Take care ma'am.

Jennifer reassures with a nod.

Older man treads.

INT. PIERRE AND JENNIFER'S HOME - SAME DAY

Broken glass. Mildew. Mold. Overturned piano. Broken kitchen cabinets. Gabriel's toys destroyed.

They barely move. HEAVY BREATHING through the mask.

> JENNIFER
> Oh my God!

Jennifer slips on muddy slush floors.

> JENNIFER
> Aah!

> PIERRE
> Hold onto the wall.

Jennifer's glove touches the wall.

> PIERRE
> Don't fall in this crap.

Her boots stick to grime.

Pierre's face reflects "trepidation."

> PIERRE
> Maybe, we can salvage some things.

Jennifer appears "mystified."

Dazed Pierre discovers his wet and molded baby photo album. He holds it and lowers his head.

Jennifer walks…

UP THE STAIRWELL…

A picture falls. Glass shatters.

> JENNIFER
> Shit!

Pierre follows…

TO THE MASTER BEDROOM…

Water drips from the ceiling. Looking through the shattered windows, a NATIONAL GUARDSMAN hangs on the side of a helicopter with a rifle in hand.

A GERMAN SOLDIER, who volunteered to help with relief efforts, speaks German through his bullhorn.

A snake slithers across the floor. Pierre cautions Jennifer with an arm across her chest.

TO GABRIEL'S ROOM…

Mold everywhere. Buzz Lightyear comforter and stuffed animals are barely visible. Hole in the ceiling… view of the sky.

Jennifer removes her mask and wipes the sweat.

>   PIERRE
> Keep it on!

>   JENNIFER
> I can't breathe.

>   PIERRE
> Don't breathe this in.

>   JENNIFER
> I don't give a shit anymore!

>   PIERRE
> Put your damn mask on!

Jennifer reluctantly obliges.

>   JENNIFER
> I've seen enough.

>   PIERRE
> Wait outside then.

Jennifer scampers…

DOWN THE STAIRCASE…

She stomps. Angrily, she rips her mask off.

EXT. PIERRE AND JENNIFER'S HOME - CONTINUOUS

Jennifer tosses the mask and piercingly screams. She rips her boots off and throws them. She yanks her white hazmat suit.

Pierre approaches. They collapse in each other's arms and bawl.

A SONG, such as "Only Love" by Ben Howard, PLAYS.
> *Darling you're with me, always around me.*
> *Only love, only love.*

Darling I feel you, under my body.
Only love, only love.
Give me shelter, or show me heart.
Come on love, Come on love.
Watch me fall apart, watch me fall apart.

Watch me fall apart, watch me fall apart,
watch me fall apart.

Coming Home

Chapter 11
Evacuation Snapshots

The older man came from nowhere. He helped and disappeared. Was he sent? An angel in disguise? He was someone we never met before—someone we may never see again. But in that short time, he arrived, willing, able, and concerned. The older man helped us and vanished. He knew what we were about to enter. He didn't need to stay for a private moment. He stayed for his purpose, and he left. And we received compassion and help in our dire moment.

» *Do you have a hard time receiving?*

» *We hear that it is better to give than receive. Many of us believe that the wonder is the "gift giver." We elevated that status to a fault.*

» *But what about receiving? Do you accept help? Do you refuse help?*

» *Do you talk yourself out of it? Too humbled? Too prideful?*

» *We live in a society that teaches giving without regard to self. We give until self-depletion… out of duty, obligation, people-pleaser mentality, "a servant's heart."*

» *Not saying "NO" when we should.*

» *Neglecting our own self-care.*

» *Neglecting our own worth.*

» *Neglecting our own value.*

» *But receiving is truly the bigger issue.*

» *How do you receive criticism?*

» *How do you receive encouragement?*

» *How do you receive that compliment?*

» *How do you receive awareness?*

» *How do you receive help from a lover, a friend, a stranger?*

» *Because it's truly in the receiving moments that the walls to your heart crumble.*

» *You realize that the universe truly is looking out for you.*

» *You are safe, secure, loved, and loving.*

» *May you receive the opportunities and teachable moments.*

» *May your heart receive all the love, joy, and peace that presents itself truly in mysterious ways.*

» *May you allow the art of receiving to rule in your heart.*

WATCH ME FALL APART

You go into situations ready and prepared. Or you think you are. But once I was there, I fell apart. I didn't want Pierre telling me what to do. I didn't want anyone telling me what to do. I wanted to weep, to feel, to grieve. Haven't you felt like that before? When no sound advice or encouragement will assist? When the words become chatter? When the noise magnifies? *I wanted to damn well feel. "This sucks! This really sucks!"*

Our destroyed den.

I felt for Gabriel. He was three at the time. All he had ever known was destroyed: his toys, his stuffed animals, his books, his room, his home. Hadn't he been through enough? Isn't enough... enough?

All we ever knew was gone.

Something we created was destroyed. That's what really hurt. *It's not about the things. It's about the creation:* rocking Gabriel in the glider throughout the night; the Hot Wheels® scattered on the floor; the kitchen, which supplied fellowship and friendship; the house that supplied guests; visitors coming and going; Pierre walking through the door with his briefcase; the kisses when he came and when he left; the routine; the organization; the safety.

It was the creation of memories: what we created in our marriage, what we created individually, and what we created in our family.

Den cabinet where Pierre found his baby book.

When you lose everything, you become completely exposed: vulnerable, transparent, and sensitive. There is no more hiding this or that. You become undone. And the undoing process creates space for something beautiful to unfold. You may not see it in that moment—the heartache is unbearable—but you get glimpses of what is to come. And I learned, "This or better." These moments are temporary... temporary infractions across the journey of life, leaving a little scar or wound for a greater depth and sensitive awareness.

- I know what it's like to be wounded and wound.
- I know what it's like to be abused and the abuser with my words.
- I know what it's to be confused and confuse.
- I know what it's it like to create and destroy.
- I know what it's like to give and receive.
- I know what it's like to struggle and let go.
- I know what it's like to run and hide.
- I know what it's like to stuff my feelings and become numb.
- *I know what it's like to be engrossed and engulfed by crushing life storms.*

Oh, how I searched high and low in the midst of pain and suffering. Where is the beauty? *I discovered it in the experience of feelings... the experience of my level of awareness.* My heart longed and my soul yearned for more expansion, more expression—more. I found it in unconditional love, forgiveness, understanding, inner peace, acceptance, compassion, letting go of the same way of experiencing life, letting in all of me.

Our dining room and living room.

Our devastated kitchen.

LIFE SCRIPTS

» *I got a feeling… "To Acknowledge Your Feelings."*

» *I can't recall anyone teaching me in childhood or adulthood to pay attention to my feelings. It was do, do, do. In school. At home. In church. I was taught feelings can mislead you. Feelings come, and feelings go. Don't trust them!*

» *Was I misled into a belief system, a conditioning, a paradigm that did not resonate with my core inner being? An emphatic yes.*

» *I stuffed, hid, and quenched my feelings for too long.*

» *By not acknowledging my feelings, I only hurt myself.*

» *What beliefs do we hold that are wrecking our lives?*

» *Doing more damage than good?*

» *When I acknowledged my feelings, a new awareness blew in like fresh air.*

» *Our feelings are our internal guidance system. They teach us if we are on the right path or not. Our feelings are meant to be acknowledged, expressed, felt.*

» *They lead you and guide you into the beauty of fullness.*

» *How do you feel on a daily basis?*

» *In your mind? In your body? In your heart? In your soul?*

» *How do you feel?*

Coming Home

Chapter 12
Playing Dirty

Pierre and I took our frustrations out on each other. We became punching bags, playing dirty at times, threats of leaving and divorce, shredding each other into thoroughly damaged pieces. We repeated the same, ingrained patterns of self-hate, patterns of abandonment, and patterns of rejection.

There are basically two feelings in the world... love and fear. *A Course in Miracles* teaches that we either express love or express fear, which is really a call to love. What Pierre and I needed was love, security, and stability in our marriage, in our finances, in our parenting, and in our circumstances. The more we projected that need on each other, the more the weaknesses of the other were magnified. I couldn't find the love that I needed in Pierre. I needed to find it in myself—in my alignment with Source, Energy, God, Spirit. And the more I aligned with the Creator instead of the creation, the more I tuned in with unconditional love, infinite possibilities, infinite intelligence, unlimited resources, and power beyond measure.

"Lord, make me an instrument of thy peace." ~ St. Francis of Assisi on The Serenity Prayer.

Peace doesn't come from our external world but our internal world. I had to go inside my violent mind to secure peace. Pierre couldn't give me that peace. Another hurricane couldn't secure that peace. Another surgery couldn't secure my peace. Another city or state couldn't secure that peace.

I discovered the inner peace within myself. It's taken me years to embrace that I had to go within to unlock the freedom of my heart and soul. I've been enslaved and chained to archaic beliefs, fear, self-doubt, and trauma—you name it! But I didn't need to stay there. I can move forward in life beautifully and magnificently, with new compassionate truths and expanded awareness. I can understand myself and my pain to understand others and their pain.

Every circumstance in our life is to return us to home. Pierre Teilhard de Chardin once said, *"We are not human beings having a spiritual experience. We are spiritual beings having a human experience."* It's a fine distinction, but one that keeps us balanced, grounded, centered. The more we align with the spiritual world, our beingness, and our knowingness, the more we can feel at rest in the physical world. Breathe that in because it's such a permeable truth that makes life easier, guided, and energized. It's tapping into Spirit, honoring our soul, and connecting with Source that frees us to truly live an abundant life!

How do I know? Because I searched for my identity and stability in others, circumstances, and situations. It left me depleted, overwhelmed, and exhausted. My identity is in the divine. My stability rests in the divine. There is nothing more to add, and surely nothing to remove. There is only an awareness, an acceptance, an alignment.

It's a response to life instead of a reaction to life. It's being the observer and the game changer. Mahatma Gandhi suggested, *"Be the change that you wish to see in the world."* It's you being the change. It's me being the change. It's a healing and clarity of the mind that ushers you into deeper truths.

It's a training, a cultivating, a process—not another testing. Can I put these new insights into action? Can I love Pierre when I have unmet expectations? *A heart in motion.* Or am I delivering lip service?

IS LOVE WORTH THE FIGHT?

We hear it in the Switchfoot song that "Love Alone is Worth the Fight." But do we believe it?

It makes me ponder love. Is it worth the fight?

We see the fairy tale in movies. We hear the lyrics that convey heartfelt emotion. We sense an attractive person in a restaurant. We feel the touch of our lover. We smell their fragrance that lingers in a room.

Do we stay in a marriage because God says?

Stay out of duty and obligation?

Stay because of fear and guilt?

Stay for the kids?

Stay for the comfort?

Stay because we are stuck in the same patterns?

Stay because we are older and scared to date?

Stay because family members and friends suggest it's the "right" thing to do?

Or do we stay because we look at those obstacles as opportunities of healing, growth, and expansion?

If we love unconditionally, then we do not need the conditions to change. Right?

I'm preaching to the choir because I've been there. I considered divorce. Pierre considered divorce. We considered divorce. What got us to that place? All the above and none of the above. We misunderstood love by making it conditional;

we wanted conditions to be the way when we were dating or early on in our marriage; we wanted the connection, acceptance, and understanding; we wanted the sense of intimacy; we wanted to be fully known and knowing; we wanted the partnership and the playmate—*wanted it to be damn different in whatever way possible!*

Can things change? Yes, in an instant... by shifting perspectives. It's a decision to shift a perspective in an instant with fresh clarity. So, what is the mindset of love?

Love is Steadfast. *It is patient.*

Love is Tender. *It is kind.*

Love is Content. *It does not envy.*

Love is Confident. *It does not boast.*

Love is Humble. *It is not proud.*

Love is Respectful. *It is not rude.*

Love is Inclusive. *It is not self-seeking.*

Love is Courageous. *It is not easily angered.*

Love is Forgiveness. *It keeps no record of wrongs.*

Love is Consistent. *It does not delight in evil.*

Love is Freedom. *It rejoices in truth.*

Love is Nearness. *It always protects.*

Love is Strength. *It always trusts.*

Love is Desirable. *It always hopes.*

Love is Diligent. *It always perseveres.*

Love is Resilient. *It never fails.*

Worth it? You're damn right—even when: every cell in your body screams otherwise; you want to run and never return; the silence between you speaks volumes of loss; especially when you crave more connection.

People grow and evolve at different rates and different seasons. Some may not evolve. *But can you still love them when they don't meet your expectations... when they don't change... when you change?!*

Tony Robbins said, *"If you treat people at the end of the relationship like the beginning, there won't be an end."* Oh, the beginning—hearts beating and uniting in intoxicating love. Then, the screeching brakes of reality hit you—patterns of dullness, sameness, and stuckness. What happened? Where did it go? Can you get it back?

What about new beginnings? New realities? New mindsets? Is it worth it? Are you worth it? What if right before you throw in the towel, the miracle is just around the corner? Is it easy? Of course not. It's a battle, warfare—a fight. Is it challenging? Everyday. But you will never know until you cross the finish line. Will you?

Something we created was destroyed. Our home was destroyed. It provided shelter. But it was more than a building. It was a shelter for love.

All that remains is love. And love can be recreated. Can't it?

Pierre and me smiling together.

Is love worth the fight? Are you worth it? Come on love.

Chapter 13
Coming Home Snapshots

Our home had seven feet of water inside. The roof blew off in some places, and it basically rained in the house. We walked around the house in a trance, taking it in, overwhelmed by the extent of the damage. We had flood damage and roof damage.

We lived in the Lakeview neighborhood in New Orleans. The 17th Street Canal broke and caused floodwaters to enter our home. The wind from Hurricane Katrina blew pieces of our roof off. Mold and mildew were rampant. It was a hot mess.

The 17th Street Canal is a drainage canal that flows into Lake Pontchartrain. The canal, along with the Orleans Canal and the London Avenue Canal, form the New Orleans Outfall Canals. The 17th Street Canal separates the city of New Orleans from Metairie, Louisiana.[21]

Our street name was New Basin Way, but we called it "New Baby Way" because there was a boom of babies in the neighborhood. There were seventeen built homes near a bomb shelter. Yes, that's right—a bomb shelter. The New Orleans Bomb

Shelter is located on the neutral ground between Pontchartrain Boulevard and West End Boulevard, just before Robert E. Lee Boulevard. It was built in the early 1950s by the City of New Orleans as a refuge for the Mayor and City Council. City officials could use the Pontchartrain Expressway (built before Interstate 10) to reach the shelter and prepare for "disasters caused by enemy attacks or other hostile action, or by fire, flood, earthquakes, or other natural causes."[22] The shelter became obsolete in the late 1950s. It ceased being maintained in the 1970s.[23]

Floodwaters from Katrina almost reached the top of our street sign.

HOME GARAGE

We didn't use our garage to park cars. We used our air-conditioned garage as Gabriel's play area. It was adjacent to my kitchen, so I could cook and enjoy the sounds of Gabriel. Pierre and I arranged it that way so he had a play area. With his Giant Pigmented Nevus, he lacked sweat glands, and New Orleans can get hot and humid. Maybe you know if you've visited.

Maybe you know if you live there. We created the garage as a play area with his fire truck. He had a playhouse with a slide, crayons and paper, and we laid indoor carpet.

Before we evacuated, we took any movable, exterior objects and stored them in the garage. Some items included our patio table, chairs, and potted plants.

Garages are stable. They protect your car. Pierre's car was parked in front of our circular driveway. His car was destroyed, nothing to salvage, just like Gabriel's belongings were destroyed, nothing to salvage.

Pierre's car parked in front of the circular driveway.

Destroyed garage with Gabriel's fire truck and toys.

The garage was Gabriel's play area.

SALVAGE

We went back and forth from the Lakeview area to the Mandeville area north of Lake Pontchartrain. Pierre rented a U-Haul® truck in Mississippi.

I couldn't go back in the house the next day. Emotionally, I'd seen enough. I stayed back with Gabriel at my parent's home in Beau Chêne. Thankfully, my parents arrived. The New Orleans Louis Armstrong International Airport was up and running. Pierre went back in our home to see what could possibly be salvaged, and my parents went with him.

My sister, Lauren, flew in from Houston to help. She claimed, "Jennifer, I even got a tetanus shot. And I don't like shots." She came prepared. My parents came prepared.

We salvaged our master bedroom, the place of rest, intimacy, and connection: the bed that we conceived Gabriel, the Sunday naps, the sleepy early mornings, the hugs, the tears, the laughter, the fun, the talks, the sharing.

My kitchen cabinets fell apart. If you touched the wood, they broke even more with everything in it. But my dad insisted on getting my wedding china, and thankfully he did.

Our paintings were destroyed: ones we purchased in Italy and France, ones we purchased at furniture stores in Baton Rouge and New Orleans, ones we purchased from a U-Haul® truck on our street. We rolled them with the hopes that they could be restored one day.

Pierre took his destroyed baby book. His lifespan flashed before his eyes. Maybe just maybe, he could see those images again.

We salvaged clothes. My mom's home became a stinky laundromat. We spent days washing and rewashing clothing. We realized that the moistness from the flood conditions would not give up their nasty smells easily. Finally, we sent them to a professional restoration dry cleaning business. They restore clothes following flood, fire, and natural disasters.

My mind was not in a good place to replace a new wardrobe. It was in a place of survival. It was how I lived life.

Once we decided to move to California, Pierre put a "for sale by owner" sign in front of our home on New Basin Way, and we left. We left all that we knew and all that we have even known, but not everything we will know.

When we evacuated, it was the last time Gabriel saw his home.

Pierre and I breathed in the devastation, the damage, the destruction from Hurricane Katrina. And we breathed out peace, anticipation, newness.

LIFE SCRIPTS
REWRITE, REDIRECT, RECREATE

» *What parts of you are for sale?*

» *The pieces of yourself that you give away.*

» *Your strength and your power. Your identity and your stability.*

» *Your alignment with Source, Energy, God, Universe.*

» *What pieces of you can be salvaged?*

» *Maybe it's clarity of mind. Maybe it's an energized body.*

» *Maybe it's a life-giving environment.*

» *Maybe it's fulfilled relationships.*

» *Perhaps, it is all of the above.*

You are worth it. Gloriously worth it. May you discover it, embrace it, and live it. You are not for sale.

Coming Home

Chapter 14
Good-Byes

We said good-byes to family and friends. Everyone was distraught. Their faces were dismal. No one could make much sense of anything. No one really understood the move to Encinitas, California.

We hopped in our green SUV, the same one we evacuated in, and sat for hours. But now it was with the eagerness and hopes of getting somewhere... to start anew.

My mom drove with us. She knew we needed help with Gabriel's upcoming surgery. As soon as we arrived in California, we had to fly to Chicago for his 11th surgery.

Stevie, Gabriel's babysitter, drove with us. She wanted to be there for support, to help with Gabriel, and to see where we were moving. Stevie knew we only had a couple of days in California before we headed to Chicago, but she was willing to drive with us anyway.

Once again we drove...
How long will I go?

Will I stay past the year?
Will I like this new place?
Will I come back to visit?
Will I come back to live?
Will I return?

RETURNING HOME AGAIN

Sometimes home is in our physical location. Sometimes it is in our memories, those places that live in your heart and carry you.

Returning Home. Does it bring you to a place of eagerness or make you distraught? Can we return to places within us? Really can we connect?

We are immensely bountiful with so many resources and gifts. There are people that teach us, encourage us, and love us. They are the strangers who smile at us on the street, the neighbor who picks up your child from school when you are in a jam, the ones who see your potential when you don't, the ones that make you meals when your son comes home from surgery. They are the people with which time can go by as if no time was ever lost. They are the ones who challenge you. They are the ones that forgive. *They are you, forgiving yourself.*

Places. I've experienced so much: dinners in Tuscany, cruising with my grandmother in North Africa, cruising with my grandpa in Turkey, standing in awe of the Eiffel Tower, experiencing the scale of the Mona Lisa in The Louvre, driving through the clean streets of Switzerland, witnessing multiple surgeries in Chicago, and seeing delightful musicals and spellbound plays in New York. So many places have touched me.

One of my favorite trips was one I made to Hawaii with my family. We kayaked and canoed as we breathed in the fresh air, enjoyed the splendor of a waterfall, and saw the delight in my boys' faces as they experienced the pure joy of the moment.

Our muddy feet after an incredible hike in Hawaii.

I've lived in Louisiana, Alabama, and California, delighting that they are different, yet unique.

I have enjoyed my mom's cooking, the smell of pralines as I came home from school, the family trips to Florida, summers swimming in Fontainebleau, the streets of Henry Clay Avenue and Magazine, the shrimp po'boys at Norby's.

Time is fleeting yet awe-inspiring.

I am bountiful with God-given resources within me... knowing that He is my strength, sufficiency, supplier, sustainer, and shield.

Home is where the heart is. Our awareness is in our emotional state. We can observe those thoughts and feelings with a sweet clarity that only comes from experiencing life fully: the ups and downs, the uncertainties, the risks, and the emotional exposure of it all.

LIFE SCRIPTS
REWRITE, REDIRECT, RECREATE

» *Have you returned to your past?*

» *Have you returned to this very present moment?*

» *Have you returned home?*

» *Have you returned to your feelings?*

» *Have you returned to your memories?*

» *Have you returned to the meaning and understanding of it all?*

» *Returned to a place of love?*

» *And honored the sanctuary that it all was, all is, and all will be?*

I'm on that journey and can honestly say it's worth it. And I will continue on this journey of clarity and healing while I vibrate with the frequency of love, peace, joy, and bliss. Each experience carries me, teaches me, and breathes new life into me. As I let go of the tight grip, I surrender to the process, to my evolution, to a gentler way of life—to a gentler way of being. Surrender. Yes, sweet surrender.

Coming Home

Chapter 15
The Awareness Of It All

Do you approve of yourself? Do you approve of your job? Do you approve of your relationships? Do you approve of your finances? Do you approve of your circumstances? Do you approve of your pain and despair? Do you approve of your life storms? Most of us have a hard time approving when times get challenging... when the eye of the hurricane lingers.

We perpetuate an unhealthy environment when the eye of the hurricane lingers... when the devastation, damage, and destruction occurs. We spew complaints and criticism, and our mindset becomes one of sabotage, scarcity, conflict, and drama. Our mindset can become our own worst enemy—we can become our own worst enemy.

How often do you criticize yourself? Be truthful because I know our human nature and our human mind. Oh, and I know myself.

We Criticize Ourselves Incessantly...

- *Because our stomach sags after childbirth.*
- *Because the wrinkles and sunspots suddenly appear.*
- *Because we neglected our self-care.*
- *Because we sought love from another instead of giving it to ourselves.*
- *Because we didn't have time to watch the latest TV episode or finish that intriguing novel.*
- *Because we corrected our children on the same issues.*
- *Because we hit the snooze button instead of waking up before the crack of dawn.*
- *Because our finances are tight.*
- *Because we didn't make it to the gym.*
- *Because we neglected our meditational or devotional practice.*
- *Because our partner forgot our anniversary... again.*
- *Because our children sassed us back in public.*
- *Because we burnt the bread.*
- *Because we slipped with that foul language.*
- *Because we didn't call that friend back who needed our help.*
- *Because we didn't plan accordingly for retirement.*
- *Because we flounder in our purpose.*
- **BUT... *What if your purpose is to approve of yourself?***

"You've been criticizing yourself for years and it hasn't worked. Try approving of yourself and see what happens." ~ Louise Hay

What an earth-shattering idea. What a life-giving concept. What a joyful and loving experience filled with amazing grace, amazing peace... amazing.

I thought to experience unconditional love, unconditional peace, and unconditional clarity was to not let the conditions dictate my reaction, my joy, my purity. I discovered that *our conditions are our perceptions... our conditions are our percep-tions.* I repeat it because it's a new thought. And faith, belief, and truth come through repetition.

What do you want to see? In every moment, you get to choose what you see. You can experience love or fear—really the bottom-line in perception!

We choose! We choose to see love or hate. We choose to experience clarity or confusion. We choose to ascertain doubt or belief. We choose our perception! We do have control. We are powerful beyond measure.

"Our deepest fear is not that we are inadequate. Our deepest fear is that we are powerful beyond measure. It is our light, not our darkness that most frightens us. We ask ourselves, Who am I to be brilliant, gorgeous, talented, and fabulous? Actually, who are you not to be? You are a child of God. Your playing small does not serve the world. There is nothing enlightened about shrinking so that other people will not feel insecure around you. We are all meant to shine, as children do. We were born to make manifest the glory of God that is within us. It is not just in some of us; it is in everyone and as we let our own light shine, we unconsciously give others permission to do the same. As we are liberated from our own fear, our presence automatically liberates others." ~ Marianne Williamson

Our perceptions create our reality. Our perceptions create our conditions. Our perceptions create our consistency, our constancy, our identity, our stability.

LIFE SCRIPTS
REWRITE, REDIRECT, RECREATE

» *What do you choose?*

» *What do you criticize yourself over?*

» *What do you approve of yourself in?*

» *What perceptions create your conditions?*

» *What reality do you choose to create?*

» *Put down your sword... of attack, of powerlessness, of a critical spirit, of fear.*

» *Pick up the pieces of your heart and choose... a healing mindset, your power and strength, an approving spirit, love.*

» *Take back your identity and your stability when the storms of life engulf you.*

HOLDING YOUR HEART

Come home. Yes, come home to your vibrant higher self, your glorious heart and soul. May you hold your heart and feel your heart beat for the very first time.

I held my heart for the first time, and I wept. It was a profound experience... to open the chambers of my heart... to be raw in my essence... to fully embody my spiritual nature as well as my physical nature. Heart to heart, hand in hand, feeling my rhythm, I lay in the grass and felt the beat of connection, compassion, clarity, courage, confidence, commitment, and cycles.

At the age of three, I sat in the grass in a blue-smocked dress with big blue eyes and fair skin. *What was I thinking? Was I carried away?* I see the face of longing—longing to know myself.

I sat in the yard with my blue-smocked dress and Mardi Gras beads.

As an adult, I walked naked across a field, clothed with the garments of love and worthiness on my back, leading with my courageous heart, softening with wings of protection, my feet planted firmly in the ground, the northern star guiding me into unchartered territory... my heart. *I was never carried away but carried along*—carried along as deep calls to deep.

It is well. I am safe, secure, loved, and loving. You are well. You are safe, secure, loved, and loving. There is nothing more to do. There is nothing to fix. When you find your authentic self... your heart... your soul, you realize that you are the only true space of coming home.

Put a new song in your heart because you are worth new beginnings, new realities, and new mindsets.

A song, such as "Come Home" by One Republic, played.

> *I get lost in the beauty*
> *Of everything I see*
> *The world ain't half as bad*
> *As they paint it to be*

If all the sons,
All the daughters
Stopped to take it in
Well hopefully the hate subsides and the love can begin
It might start now, yeah
Well maybe I'm just dreaming out loud
Until then...

Come home
Come home
Cause I've been waiting for you
For so long
For so long

You have never been carried away. You were always carried along. Come home.

The Move
Life Scripts Four

FADE IN:

EXT. SAN DIEGO INTERNATIONAL AIRPORT - LATE
EVENING

SUPER: "SAN DIEGO INTERNATIONAL AIRPORT"

Jennifer and Pierre appear weary as they wait
at baggage claim. Gabriel sleeps on Jennifer's
shoulder.

STEVE HUFFMAN, tall, debonair, big smile,
dressed in nice slacks and tailored shirt,
approaches them.

> STEVE
> I'm so glad you guys made it. Steve
> Huffman.

He shakes Pierre's hand.

> PIERRE
> Sorry about the delay. Snow in
> Philadelphia.

Steve's "compassionate" face reassures him.

> STEVE
> You guys must be exhausted.

Jennifer positions Gabriel higher.

> JENNIFER
> Thank you for helping us.

> STEVE
> I can't imagine what you guys have been
> through.

> JENNIFER
> It's all we know.

Steve extends a "concerned" look.

>STEVE
>Let's get you home.

Steve grabs their suitcase.

>STEVE
>I'll be back here in a few hours
>to drop Paige off.

IN THE CAR...

Pierre sits in passenger seat while Steve
drives.

Steve hand motions to landmarks.

>STEVE
>Great grocery. Reasonable.

Jennifer gazes through the window.

>STEVE
>This is a safe neighborhood.
>I would raise my kids here.

Car clock reads: *"1:13 a.m."*

>STEVE
>A lot of information, especially at
>this time.

>PIERRE
>We're really grateful.

>STEVE
>My heart was torn. And I'm just an
>observer.

Steve places his hand over his heart.

> STEVE
> I wasn't inclined to write a check. I
> wanted to meet a family and understand
> their story.

Steve appears "peaceful and pleased."

> STEVE
> And here you are.

> JENNIFER
> I didn't think my e-mail went through.

Steve raises his voice.

> STEVE
> I thought no one would take my offer!

Jennifer smiles.

> JENNIFER
> We always wanted to move to California.

Steve is "jolted."

> PIERRE
> Who would have thought… a hurricane!?

EXT. POINSETTIA RIDGE APARTMENT - SAME EVENING

Steve opens the apartment door to unit 247.

PAIGE HUFFMAN, cheery, beach tousled hair,
purple nail polish, hits the ants on the
counter with a towel.

Steve gives a "surprise" look.

> STEVE
> I see.

Paige giggles. Her face beams.

                    PAIGE
They're attracted to the sugar on the
donuts.
         (to PIERRE AND JENNIFER)
I'm so glad you guys are here!

She enthusiastically tosses her hands in the
air.

                    JENNIFER
Glad to settle down.

                    STEVE
They moved *thirteen times*.

                    PAIGE
Um.

Paige rubs Gabriel's back.

                    PAIGE
Aww… Look at this sleepy guy.

                    STEVE
Paige and her friends assembled
this in a week.

Paige opens the kitchen cabinets.

                    PAIGE
We got a Crock-Pot®, wok, a bread
machine.

Hand-sketched pictures of Pierre, Jennifer,
and Gabriel reside on refrigerator magnets.

Screen reveals: *"Welcome to California."*

                    JENNIFER
Adorable.

                    PAIGE
          My friend made those.

Paige opens the refrigerator door.

                    PAIGE
          We stocked the fridge. Got some items
          for Gabriel.

                    STEVE (O.S.)
          Friends donated the furniture.

Paige exudes boundless energy.

                    PAIGE
          Come see Gabriel's room.

                    STEVE (O.S.)
                 (to PIERRE)
          Gift cards to Home Depot®, Macy's®, gas
          stations.

Jennifer is in "awe" as they continue…

TO GABRIEL'S ROOM...

Bright, cheery. Buzz Lightyear comforter.
Mickey Mouse® rests on his bed.

                    JENNIFER
          How did you --

Jennifer's face softens.

                    PAIGE
          Steve asked Pierre.

Gabriel wakes up and rubs his eyes.

                    JENNIFER
          We're here.

His face lights up.

                    GABRIEL
          Buzz Lightyear!

Steve glances at Paige.

                    STEVE
          Why don't we let them get settled?!

Steve hands Pierre his car keys.

                    STEVE
          I'll check in tomorrow.

Pierre appears "baffled."

                    PIERRE
          You guys have done so much.

Steve possess a carefree style.

                    STEVE
          Just return it after you buy a car. No
          rush.

Pierre's face is in "awe."

                    PIERRE
          I don't know --

                    STEVE
          You're putting pieces of your life
          back together. That's enough.

Pierre extends his hand.

Steve grabs him and hugs him.

The Move

Chapter 16
The Visit

Steve and Paige Huffman flew us to California for a week while we were displaced. They wanted us to see everything... to experience things first hand... to meet them.

We felt like we were literally put through the wringer. Yet, everything seemed calm and peaceful in California. Like life just went on. For us, life was interrupted by Hurricane Katrina. We were trying to achieve a sense of normalcy—stability if that was even possible. We felt like we arrived in Disneyland®. Everything was clean and orderly.

Gabriel enjoyed his new friend, Mickey Mouse.®

Gabriel goofed off with Buzz Lightyear.

We wanted a place to lay our heads. We wanted rest—rest for our weary hearts and rest for our weary souls.

The Huffmans made us feel so welcomed. We were overwhelmed by their generosity, their kindness, and their enthusiasm. We weren't a burden to them. They didn't just set us in an apartment. They pursued us, checked on us, and loved us in a deep, meaningful way during our agony and loss.

After the week in Encinitas, California, we packed up the car in Louisiana and headed west. We decided to make California our home for a year. We didn't have any plans afterwards. It didn't make any sense in an analytical and linear way, but it made sense in a knowing and intuitive way.

Truthfully, it was the best experience for us at the time. If we would have stayed in Louisiana, we would have continued on a downward spiral, especially with Gabriel's upcoming surgery. We needed a break. We needed a breather. We didn't have the strength to rebuild New Orleans at the time. We were barely rebuilding our lives.

From a tragic experience, a friendship was birthed. We are still friends with Steve and Paige ten years later. They helped us get back on our feet. They set Gabriel up in school. They loaned us their car. Pierre met with Steve to discuss the insurance claims. I joined Paige and her dear friends for book club. We met for dinners and discovered new restaurants along the way. We smiled again.

ARRIVING

We were exhausted from the drive. We unloaded the U-Haul® and got settled with the items that we salvaged. Stevie ventured to Legoland® with Gabriel.

I ran to the grocery and used my EBT card for the first time. We had one for a few months following the hurricane. I had never used food stamps before. It was a humbling experience indeed.

I unloaded the items on the conveyor belt. The cashier wore a tongue ring and heavy black eyeliner. She was not a happy camper as she slurred, "Paper or plastic?" I inquired, "Can I pay with an EBT card?" For some reason, it had a gentler connotation versus food stamps, especially with people lined up behind me. The cashier pursued the obvious, "Food stamps?" I nodded yes. Then I felt responsible to explain myself: "Survivor of Hurricane Katrina." The cashier gave a look that said, "Who really gives a shit!" She replied, "Yea... We accept food stamps." I passed her my EBT card. The cashier flippantly said, "You made out pretty good. I need a hurricane." I quickly responded, "You make do with your circumstances."

I was embarrassed. I felt like I had to explain.

Yes, I'm a Hurricane Katrina survivor. But I survived so much more. I never was and never will be a victim. Victimhood takes away your power. And my adventure of life was leading me and guiding me to strength, courage, and power.

LIFE SCRIPTS
REWRITE, REDIRECT, RECREATE

» *How often do we... explain ourselves, defend ourselves, promote ourselves?*

» *Offer more than suggested... more than needed... more than anyone deem care?*

» *No one can sit in judgment of you. No one can sit in judgment of your life. No one can sit in judgment, unless you allow them.*

» *There is nothing to explain. And sometimes the more we explain, the deeper the hole of desperation we crawl into.*

» *Don't give your power away. You are who you are. There is nothing to be ashamed of... your sad and bright past, your uncomfortable and wonderful present, or your anxious and delightful future.*

» *Do you need a hurricane to feel good, to experience life fully, to flourish?*

» *What circumstances do you need to awaken and usher you into greatness, not smallness?*

Yes, I had an EBT card—thankfully. It's the most government assistance we received besides the $2,000 FEMA check.

Yes, it took a hurricane to awaken me, along with my other life storms. In fact, it has taken all my life experiences to heal me—heal my wounded heart, my self-esteem, my self-worth, my shattered pieces.

I used to believe that I had to "fix myself." *"Go fix Jennifer" was my mantra of the day. But I discovered that I found Jennifer instead.* I wasn't a project to fix, an item to check off my to-do list, a renovation to endure. If there is no fixing, then there is no self-improvement. Right?! It's a road, a path, a journey of self-discovery, self-awareness, self-love, self-care, self-worth, self-empowerment, and self-validation!

It's finding, discovering, and exploring all of me that led to my greatest comfort. Reassurance of a gentle whisper that everything is all right. Everything will be all right. There is nothing to fear.

Rumi pontificated, *"Your task is not to seek for love, but merely to seek and find all the barriers within yourself that you have built against it."*

I had so many walls. I lived in fear, guilt, and shame. Year after year, I piled more negative emotions into my emotional dump truck. I felt suppressed and depressed. My voice was silenced. Afraid to speak, I was raised in a family that didn't discuss serious issues. I married a man that wanted to protect me with the same belief. Let's not talk about these issues. I piled on more fear, guilt, and shame.

Was I enough? Am I too much? Do I need to play small? Dumb myself down so others will like me? Follow the crowd in trivial and meaningless pursuits? I internalized. Oh, I internalized.

Where I was...

The mask that I wore was a people pleaser: saying yes when I wanted to say no. I was a perfectionist at everything externally, yet crumbling internally all too often. The mask that I wore was a dutiful wife, yet I was bored and restless, longing for the adventure of partnership. I accepted the roles of society to be loyal and a team player.

I wore masks for my family, my husband, other moms at school, my church. The masks that I wore kept me from experiencing all of life. Parts of me were quenched by the silence, longing to be understood and accepted for who I am instead of what I should be.

The masks that I wore. Yes, wore!!!

Where I am today...

I'm fearless, daring, courageous, confident, yet misunderstood at times.

When I removed the masks, I appreciate all the beauty that's within me. When I empty myself and bare my soul and heart, I return to me. I removed my masks for my authentic self to be revealed: aligned with Source—aligned with me. *Now, I no longer wear masks.*

LIFE SCRIPTS
REWRITE, REDIRECT, RECREATE

» *Will you consider the possibility that you wear a mask?*

» *Will you consider being vulnerable?*

» *Shedding that old pattern that no longer serves you?*

» *What masks do you wear?*

» *Who are you when the masks are removed?*

» *The better question…*

» *Why do we wear them for so long?*

The Move

Chapter 17
Surgery

My mom, Pierre, and I flew to Chicago. Gabriel was scheduled for his 11th surgery to insert tissue expanders. We knew the routine. We knew the drill.

We stayed at The Belden-Stratford Hotel in Chicago, Illinois for each surgery. The hotel staff knew our family. We still receive Christmas cards from the front desk clerk, Mrs. Timothea, to this day.

The hospital days were long—the nights longer. Morphine was administered for Gabriel's agonizing pain. Gabriel stayed a night or two in the hospital. It was all our insurance company allowed for his hospital stay. The other seven to ten nights were back at The Belden-Stratford.

Family members came for support. My parents came to the first six surgeries. However, one day the time came. They approached us and said, "We need a break. We want to be grandparents again. Can Pierre's family help?" I understood my parents' request. They didn't want Gabriel to associate them with the pain. Pierre had that same sentiment. It crushed Pierre every time he stuck Gabriel with the needle to fill the tissue expanders. Pierre didn't want Gabriel to resent him for being the "needle man."

We sat in the waiting room of Chicago Memorial Hospital. Gabriel wore the blue hospital gown with teddy bears. He played Nintendo® Mario GameCube. He maneuvered the controller like a pro. It was a great distraction.

I nudged Pierre when Dr. Bauer approached us with a concerned countenance. Dr. Bauer expressed, "I'm so sorry for your loss." Pierre replied, "It could always be better... it could always be worse." I added, "We're alive and safe." Gabriel turned his head and made eye contact with Dr. Bauer. And then the sweet sound rolled off his tongue. Gabriel said, "Dr. Bauer, I love you." Dr. Bauer was taken back; it was an emotional moment. There we were for another surgery. There we were after Hurricane Katrina. There we were... moving forward, not understanding why or how, but pressing onto something different... something better. Don't you wish someone would say I love you? Sometimes we need to hear those words.

Dr. Bauer asked, "Would you guys like to postpone surgery?" Pierre revealed, "Indefinitely... But we're here." Dr. Bauer knew it was a lot: the strain us on emotionally, mentally, relationally, and physically. It was our normal. It was all we were experiencing. Dr. Bauer genuinely encouraged, "You guys are *warriors*!"

Just another life storms to navigate.

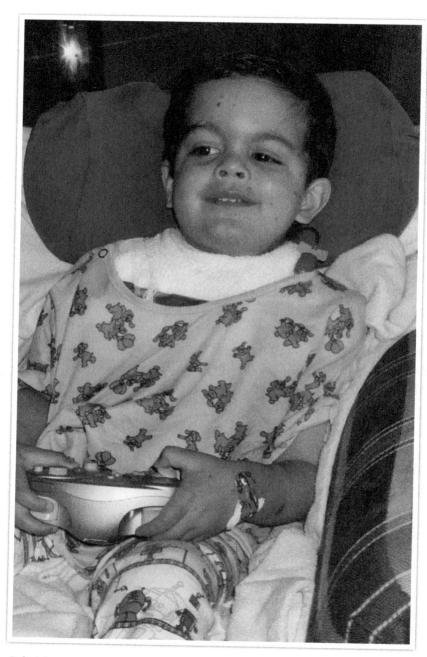

Gabriel maneuvered his game controller after surgery.

» *What distracts you?*

» *What distracts you from showing up differently in life?*

» *What distracts you from living the life of your dreams?*

» *What distracts you from truly thriving, not just surviving?*

» *What distracts you from experiencing joy?*

» *What distracts you from your alignment?*

» *What distracts you from connecting with your authentic self?*

The best news was yet to come. Dr. Bauer questioned, "I would like your permission to change things… if need be in the operating room?" I curiously asked, "Why?" Dr. Bauer expounded, "The purpose of the surgeries is to decrease the melanocytic load and remove the biggest concern from Gabriel's back. And we accomplished the bulk." Pierre rested his hand on Dr. Bauer's shoulder. He asserted, "This hasn't been easy, but we trust you with surgery #11 as we did with surgery #1." I studied Dr. Bauer's face. His wheels were spinning. Finally came the climax: Dr. Bauer revealed, "I may not insert tissue expanders but do serial excisions this go around." My mom yelled, "Thank God!" And she wept. I grabbed my heart.

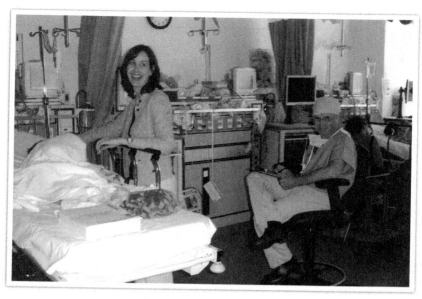

Dr. Bauer made notes in his chart while I rubbed Gabriel after surgery. Gabriel's medical chart on the hospital bed told his story of numerous surgeries.

LIFE SCRIPTS
REWRITE, REDIRECT, RECREATE

» *Do you need a break?*
» *Do you need compassion?*
» *Do need to hear the simple words, "I love you."*
» *Simplicity, compassion, and love can melt a heart of stone.*

This was going to be Gabriel's most serious surgery. A tissue expander was to be inserted in his belly. There would be three months of weekly to bi-weekly injections with saline with the intention of stretching his skin. The second part of this surgery involved a microvascular flap. The new skin would be removed from Gabriel's belly and placed on his neck. It was intense. Gabriel would be in ICU for a few days. There was a chance that his body would reject it. Gabriel would have a scar on his belly too.

Dr. Bauer showed compassion. He knew we needed a break even though we showed up. Gabriel needed a break. We just drove from Louisiana to California. Then we jumped on a plane to Chicago.

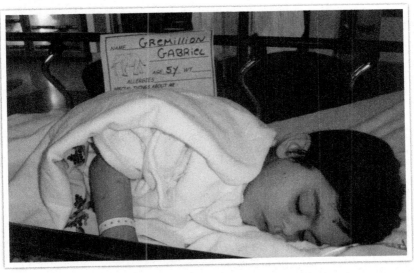

At the age of five, we decided this will be Gabriel's last surgery. Gabriel can decide "if" and "when" the next surgery will be.

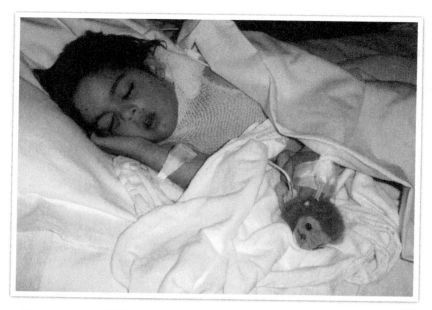

Gabriel recovered. The redness on his face revealed the effects of morphine.

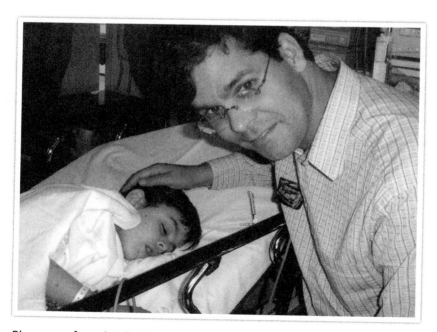

Pierre comforted Gabriel in the post-recovery unit.

I always thought of myself as a survivor—but a warrior?

Isn't perception interesting? You can think one thing in a moment while a person can view it from a different point of view. Neither person is right or wrong. They are different yet unique perspectives, bringing diversity, clarity, connection.

All experiences are another life storm to navigate. Sometimes you are on the cruise ship while other times you are on the battleship. Either way, it steers you in uncharted territory seamlessly... through the calm... through the storm. In every high... in every low, you are safe, secure, loved, and loving. There is nothing to fret over. There is only an acceptance of the present moment—letting go of the tight grip and letting in a gentler approach to life.

The Move

Chapter 18
Beach

Back in California, beach enthusiasts enjoyed another day at the beach. Surfers rode the waves. Children frolicked.

Pierre and I breathed in and let go. Gabriel emptied his bucket and filled it with sand. I drew a heart in the sand with my fingers.

A volleyball rolled near Pierre. He picked it up and tossed it back.

A song, such as "Beautiful Things" by Gungor, played.

> *All this pain*
> *I wonder if I'll ever find my way*
> *I wonder if my life could really change at all*
> *All this earth*
> *Could all that is lost ever be found*
> *Could a garden come up from this ground at all*
>
> *You make beautiful things*
> *You make beautiful things out of the dust*

You make beautiful things
You make beautiful things out of us

You are making me new

All your pain is being used for a greater purpose, a greater expansion, a greater expression. It's being cultivated into a fertile, solid soil: a strong foundation. Weeds need to be pulled from your garden. Seeds need to be planted in your garden. A lush garden will bloom. Beautiful things are made from the despair, chaos, and suffering. Beautiful things are made from the joy, order, and celebration. You are being made anew, moment by moment. You are transforming and evolving into more of the elaborate divine qualities. And your divine DNA is truly magnificent. You have the spark of the divine in you. He is the Creator. And He has created you. It's up to you to co-create your reality. It's up to you to see the beauty in the pain. It's up to you to see the beauty instead of the ashes. You are changing, and it's amazing.

Pierre and Gabriel built a sand castle at Moonlight State Beach.

Pierre and Gabriel enjoyed the Pacific Ocean.

» *What weeds need to be pulled from your garden?*

» *What seeds need to be planted in your garden?*

» *What beautiful things do you see in your garden?*

» *Do you recognize your spiritual DNA as divine and glorious?*

» *Have you accepted that you are a spiritual being?*

» *Having these physical experiences?*

In the moments of resistance, you decide... you choose... you awaken to something truly beautiful... your story. You are writing your life. Make it big. Make it count. You are gloriously worth it.

The Move

Chapter 19
California Snapshots

Rita, my mother-in-law, lost her home and her daycare business during Hurricane Katrina. She sank into a major depression. Pierre's family did not jump at the opportunity to help their mom, but I did. Since the Huffmans had three apartments in Encinitas, we took one. Rita took the second apartment with the hope that her brother would join her.

Rita arrived despondent. She touched the succulent wreath on the apartment door and asked, "Is this real?" I delighted, "Yes. Everything grows here." "Unbelievable" was her response. Gabriel was so excited that his grandma would spend the year in California with him. He proceeded, "Wait till you see the inside." He unlocked the door. Pierre, Rita, and myself followed behind him.

The décor consisted of a black kitchen table and chairs, Monet and Picasso framed posters, a cream couch, a TV on a black stand, a black office desk and chair, and bric-a-brac.

Gabriel lifted his hand, "Ta-da!" Rita raised her sunglasses. Pierre revealed, "And we're next door. Rita voiced in a sharp tone, "Lucky me." Gabriel suggested, "I can cheer you up now." But she settled on the couch and sobbed—no cheering up. Gabriel was confused. He asked, "You don't like it?" Rita expounded, "It's just that I lost my house and day-care business." Gabriel voiced, "But you're alive, and you have us. And everything you need." Gabriel hand motioned to the surroundings. Rita gave a look that said, "I know." Pierre followed, "Stop focusing on what you lost." Rita shared, "But you guys have been through so much." I added, "We all have."

"If you make your relationship with your Inner Being, your top priority… you will consistently offer the greatest advantage to others with whom you interact. Only when you are aligned with your Source, do you have anything to offer another. If your behavior is influenced by your desire to keep another person happy, you will lose your Connection to your Source. And it is not possible for you to be happy unless you are in alignment with your Source. Without that alignment, you have nothing to offer another." ~ Abraham

As you stay in alignment, you won't be thrown off course, off kilter, off balance by another's reaction, mood, or negative energy.

Oh, how I gave my power away, willingly, energetically, trying to please another… trying to get another to laugh or smile… trying to make someone else happy. And you know what it did? It made me very unhappy. Because in those moments I gave my power away, I became powerless. It was a vicious cycle, wanting to please, wanting so much more, wanting the best for someone else. I was left wanting: wanting someone to be different, wanting conditions to be different, wanting circumstances to be different.

LIFE SCRIPTS
REWRITE, REDIRECT, RECREATE

» *When was the last time you cheered someone up?*

» *Was it received easily? Was it ignored adamantly?*

» *Were you cursed for your encouragement?*

» *Were you told to leave?*

» *Did it fall on deaf ears?*

» *Maybe they just couldn't hear you because they aren't at the same level of awareness, on the same frequency, on the same vibration,*

» *Or in alignment with Source.*

I longed for a playmate. I played tennis with Pierre when we were dating over twenty years ago. We got in an argument. And guess what? We never played again. *Wanting.*

I longed for Pierre to welcome my help in buying stylish clothes. Instead, he returned them or never wore them. *Wanting.*

I longed for the fun adventure of taking dance classes, reading books together. *Wanting.*

I longed for my grandma to change her dietary choices. But her diabetes progressed anyway. *Wanting.*

I longed for Gabriel to stop playing video games excessively and connect with family and friends. *Wanting.*

I longed for weekly family devotions. *Wanting.*

See, the more I longed... the more I wanted... the more I desired... the further I got away from my connection to God, Source, Spirit. There is nothing wrong with the longing, wanting, and desire. *But I was focused on what I do not have instead of what I do have.*

I was no different than a puppet on a string trying to perform… trying to please… trying to fix. Oh, how my mantra for the day, *"Go fix Jennifer,"* extended into others' lives too, whether they wanted my help or not. I thought I had so much to give. But I wasn't received. *And when I wasn't received, I felt misunderstood.* When you understand someone, you appreciate them. And when you appreciate someone, you understand them.

What did I want? What did I long for? Alignment. I needed to stay in alignment when everyone else was out of alignment. I needed to stay in alignment for my own sake and sanity. My alignment became of upmost importance to me.

"Not only does the thought you are choosing right now attract the next thought and the next… and so on – it also provides the basis of your alignment with your Inner Being. As you consistently and deliberately think and speak more of what you do want and less of what you do not want, you will find yourself more often in alignment with the pure, positive essence of your own Source; and under those conditions, your life will be extremely pleasing to you."
~ Abraham

A belief forms from a habitual thought. What you give your attention and focus towards actually manifests. I wanted to manifest beauty, fun, order, discipline, joy, love, inner peace, and memories. I had to move in the direction of mastery of my life, not be tossed to and fro, not scattered, not leave things up to chance but conscious choices. You choose everyday: what you eat, what clothes you will wear, what music you will listen to, if you skip or take a shower, if you stay up late or are early to bed… *how you react!*

We don't live by chance. We live by conscious choices. There in that truth lies your strength and power. May you live fully alive as you make conscious choices. You are right in the *center* of where you need to be.

I surrendered. I gave up trying to make everyone else happy and chose to make myself happy. Misery may love company, but I chose not to hang out with the miserable. I chose like-minded and supportive people. I chose adventure lovers, book readers, yoga enthusiasts, health deciders, imagination movers, nature seekers. I chose me! I awoke to my voice, my feelings, my worth, my value, my passions, my patterns. I became alive. I became aware. I aligned. *"Awaken, Aliveness, Awareness, Alignment"* became my new mantra. Thankfully.

"To be alive is the biggest fear humans have. Death is not the biggest fear we have; our biggest fear is taking the risk to be alive - the risk to be alive and express what we really are. Just being ourselves is the biggest fear of humans. We have learned to live our lives trying to satisfy other people's demands. We have learned to live by other people's points of view because of the fear of not being accepted and of not being good enough for someone else." ~ Don Miguel Ruiz

You do not need someone, some place, or something to validate your worth. You are gloriously worthy... behind your hidden shadow and your marvelous light that wants to burst forth; you are worthy... beautifully flawed and shining brightly. You are worthy.

APARTMENTS

Our apartments were adjacent to one another. Rita watched a lot of TV. She listened to a lot of radio and books on tape. Since Gabriel was her heart and soul, she ventured with him on scooter rides, watched him swim in the pool, and took him to the library.

Gabriel enjoyed his bike ride around Poinsettia Ridge Apartments.

People came to visit us in Encinitas too. Friends and family members checked on us. Curiosity drove them, and they wanted to make sure we were settled.

But it wasn't all hunky-dory. Pierre fought the insurance companies on the hurricane claims. Since our apartment was noisy, Pierre made a workstation in his mom's apartment. He would treat it like he was going to the office when he really went next door. Maybe it was a simple mental shift.

Other family members took in my aunt and grandma. Aunt Anna moved in with my sister, Lauren, in Texas. My grandma resided with my parents in Mandeville. Everyone was scattered in different states, trying to make the most of the circumstances.

My little sister got engaged. Lauren asked, "Can you help plan my wedding... in San Diego?" What a kicker. I just moved to California. I had less than four months to put this shindig together. But it was a good distraction for me and Rita. It gave us something to do. It gave us a fun time of exploring the streets, and it gave Pierre quiet time to work. We explored the city of San Diego. We planned a wedding.

LIFE SCRIPTS
REWRITE, REDIRECT, RECREATE

» *Where would you like to explore?*

» *Maybe, you are waiting for someone else to join.*

» *But many times, you may continue waiting.*

» *What are you waiting for?*

» *Go explore. Have fun. Express joy. Laugh more. Dance a little or a lot.*

The Move

Chapter 20
Living In The Uncertainty

We received an offer on our home back in New Orleans on Thanksgiving Day. Someone had the strength and stamina to rebuild. We were glad that chapter closed. We were ready to build roots in California.

Pierre flew back and forth from Louisiana to California, working the best he possibly could. He commuted to Los Angeles, taking on new cases.

But we always wondered, *should we stay or should we go?* We always wanted to move to California, and it took a hurricane to get us there. Was it a conscious choice? Or was it an opportunity of positioning us, answering a desire of our hearts?

Something was still missing in our lives. Pierre and I didn't want one child. We wanted more. But it never felt like the right time to get pregnant again. I was under too much stress, and I didn't want to be pregnant in that state. I had enough anxiety over the "what ifs," and my mind could play that chatter all day long.

Our home wasn't complete. Our family wasn't complete.

Gabriel was five at the time. At a red light, Gabriel said, "Mom, I will carry the baby in my belly for you." He sensed it.

The end of the year came to a closure. Pierre and I decided to move forward, and we purchased a home in Encinitas. We intended "This or better" and manifested better.

Even though things appeared settled, we were not settled in our relationship, in our marriage, or in our finances. It was a beautiful place, but we were a hot mess, forcing things and trying harder. We didn't find that flow yet.

Our spirits were still restless.

Something was missing.

LIFE SCRIPTS
REWRITE, REDIRECT, RECREATE

» *Is there ever a right time when you have everything perfectly lined up?*

» *To move, to accept the new position, to purchase a home, to get pregnant?*

» *What if everything is perfect in the imperfection?*

» *What if everything is perfect?*

I lived trying to make things perfect. But what I learned is they already are perfect. It is living in the uncertainty and accepting the present that I am certain. The uncertainty may be in the externals, but the certainties are found in the internals. If you want to live a life of bliss, dwell on the certainties of joy, unconditional love, inner peace, courage, and strength. They are your treasures. You just have to open the treasure box.

I penned, "What is the meaning of life?" in my journal at the age of 15, searching for and seeking answers. I learned to love unconditionally and receive love unconditionally. I'm loving and I'm loved.

My journey of trials and triumphs have led me to wonderful discoveries. Many times, I wished that someone would give me that golden nugget. But truly, it's more breathtaking and life-giving when you go through the process and discover it yourself. You want to dig in the treasure box like a child. Then, the revealed path comes to you—that's the biggest treasure!

I've learned so much. And I'm still learning on this healing and clarifying path.

Here's what I got so far.... Ready to dig with me in the treasure chest?

TREASURES OF LIFE:

~ Question your beliefs.

~ Enjoy the beauty of nature.

~ Let go of the past, people, and patterns.

~ Perspective. Perspective. Perspective.

~ Heal old wounds. Love from wholeness.

~ Be open and flexible to all possibilities. You may welcome an unexpected opportunity.

~ There is no lack, only abundance.

~ Be transparent and authentic.

~ Have compassion for yourself.

~ Live in the present moment.

~ Awaken. Awareness. Alignment.

~ Serve from a generous and willing heart.

~ The power of oneness.

~ There is nothing to fear.

~ Follow your heart.

~ Choose joy.

~ Trusts your instincts.

~ Breathe.

~ Speak the language of the universe: frequency, energy, and vibration.

~ Contentment attracts more contentment.

~ Stop judging.

~ Go after your dreams.

~ Dance and sing.

~ Attitude is everything.

~ Meditation opens the door to meaning, beauty, and discovery.

~ Take inspired action, not any action.

~ There are many approaches, journeys, and roads, but only one destination.

~ Return to home. Return to love. Return to joy.

~ Timeless. Limitless. Boundless.

~ Surround yourself with encouraging people.

~ Open your heart to receiving.

~ Offer yourself forgiveness and extend it to others.

~ Love unconditionally. Share it. Extend it. Give it. Create it.

~ Understand the subtle difference between shame and guilt, and embrace compassion for yourself.

~ Have gratitude for all the moments, lessons, challenges, victories, and experiences.

~ Bust open the door of exploration, discovery, and growth.

~ God is Source. God is Energy. God is Being. God is Knowing. God is Love.

~ Patience. Welcome the rhythm, seasons, and cycles.

~ Inner peace cannot be shaken.

~ You create your reality.

LIFE SCRIPTS
REWRITE, REDIRECT, RECREATE

» *What have you discovered?*

» *What have you learned?*

» *What are you learning?*

» *What lights you up?*

» *What turns you on?*

» *What is the meaning of your life?*

» *Dig in the treasure box to discover the greatest treasure... YOU!*

» *The relationship with yourself is paramount. Life-giving. The game-changer.*

» *May your path light up with brilliance and sparkles. May it be revealed to you.*

» *Welcome the biggest treasure: you, your path, your purpose.*

Sweet Illumination
Life Scripts Five

FADE IN:

INT. KITCHEN - DAY

Gabriel, 5, lies on the kitchen floor with two tissue expanders in his neck.

> GABRIEL
> Oww. Oww. It hurts.

Jennifer administers pain medicine.

> JENNIFER
> I know. One more week.

> GABRIEL
> I don't want any more surgeries.
> I want to swim, ride a bike, play
> outside, like the other kids.

Jennifer sits next to Gabriel and rubs his arm.

> JENNIFER
> You'll do that and more.

> GABRIEL
> And I want a brother and sister… My
> best friend for life. Who gets me and
> wants to play with me.

> JENNIFER
> I understand.

Jennifer kisses his forehead.

> GABRIEL
> I love God with all my heart, soul, and
> mind. As much as I love God, I want a
> brother and a sister.

PHONE RINGS.

                    GABRIEL
          That bad!

He holds her hand tightly.

                    GABRIEL
          It hurts! It hurts!

Gabriel squirms.

                    ANSWERING MACHINE (V.O.)
          Leave a message after the beep and
          we'll call you back.

                    DANIELLE (V.O.)
          I found your baby.

Sweet Illumination

Chapter 21
We Always Knew

I met Pierre at his law office. I worked for my dad as a law clerk the summer before I attended law school. Pierre and my dad rented office space from the same building. I didn't plan to date anyone at the office. It just happened.

My dad approached me, "I think Pierre likes you." Once my dad brought it to my attention; I noticed too. Pierre was always around... always available... always interested. He asked me out on our first date. But Pierre was so tired that he even asked me to drive. I thought, *This is a first.* We went to Charley G's restaurant. He ordered a cappuccino to stay awake and a screwdriver cocktail to loosen up... at the same time.

Pierre wasn't like the other guys I dated. He was extremely kind, compassionate, gentle, and patient. I was enamored with his divine inner being. He was solid and steadfast, dependable and honest. No ulterior motives. Refreshing and endearing.

By our third date, we knew we would marry. I know. It was moving along quickly.

Backstory...

A few months before we met, Pierre compiled a list of all the attributes he wanted in a woman, best friend, and wife. He prayed and turned it over to God. And then I walked through the door. He showed me the list and said, "I prayed for you. And here you are."

We both knew what we wanted. We are decisive, and yes, stubborn at times.

I was twenty-three years old at the time, and Pierre was twenty-seven. We shared a banana spilt at an ice cream parlor. I questioned, "How do you know you want to marry me?" Pierre gasped. He responded, "Because you're smart, gorgeous, fun, have a great body, decisive, independent, powerful, compassionate, and you eat a lot." Ice-cream dripped from my chin. We laughed as Pierre wiped it from me. Pierre expounded, "And that twinkle in your eyes. I see the sunflower in your blue-green eyes." I beamed and replied, "I want kids though. Not one. Maybe two or three." Pierre shared, "Me too." I elaborated, "And I want to adopt one day." Pierre added, "You never told me that." I pursued, "What? You changed your mind now?!" Pierre nodded no. He pondered, "It confirms how amazing you are." I smiled and said, "You're not too bad yourself." I kissed him from across the table. Pierre held my hand tenderly. He continued, "I knew that I would adopt one day. What I didn't know if I would find a woman that would."

Some things can't be explained. They must be felt and experienced with the heart. Pierre and I were united for a greater purpose. Years have gone by and you can lose sight of that vision. Things can get murky. But those moments are reminders to revisit—to see that it is worth it... in the beginning, in the middle, and in the end. You can't get around trials and challenges. You must go through them. They are there to transform you and transcend you.

LIFE SCRIPTS
REWRITE, REDIRECT, RECREATE

> » *What experiences need to be remembered?*
>
> » *What moments need to be revisited?*
>
> » *What experiences need to be shared but not relived?*
>
> » *What experiences awaken you?*
>
> » *What vision do you see for your life?*

IT TOOK A HURRICANE

Pierre and I started the adoption process through a fost-adopt agency. We planned to adopt a five-year-old girl through a foster care agency. We were excited. Yet something didn't quite feel right. The lady in charge of the agency came over to our home complaining about things in her own life. I offered words of encouragement. But when she left, it didn't seem like a professional relationship.

The agency called us every day. They admitted that they had an infant with HIV or hepatitis C for us to take in. I realized that they weren't listening to our needs and desires. Yes, I could take an infant with HIV or hepatitis C. My concern was for Gabriel. Would this be a good fit? Would I subject him to other conditions? And truthfully, I wanted to know what it was like to have a healthy child... not to live at doctor appointments and hospital visits. I wanted a different experience. Pierre wanted a different experience. Not because one is better than the other; it was just the desire of our heart at the time.

One day, Pierre and I prayed and fasted. We came to the same conclusion that this wasn't the agency for us. In fact, the phone stopped ringing. The agency received the same message from the universe and never called us again.

Then, my friend called. "I found your baby." Nothing else needed to be expressed.

We waited. We were positioned to receive. We removed all obstacles in the way of what we thought should be... to the way it was meant to be. It was a boy. An infant. My heart leaped. My heart knew. My heart felt him.

Sometimes, we just need to get out of the way and allow things to unfold. When they unfold, it is effortless: no figuring it out or pressing a button to make it happen, no forcing, no struggle, only a relaxed awareness—a flow to the natural rhythm of life.

LIFE SCRIPTS
REWRITE, REDIRECT, RECREATE

» *Don't you want that relaxed awareness?*

» *Don't you desire it?*

» *To move through life graceful like a gazelle?*

» *Don't you desire the flow?*

» *Don't you desire abundance, alignment, and the art of allowing?*

» *Where do you need to position yourself?*

» *What are you waiting for?*

» *What is your heart's desire?*

It's a misaligned belief to think that life has to be unyielding and challenging. With an increased awareness, you can shift that energy—shatter that belief and take on a new belief that is more powerful. One that utters freedom! Return to yourself and set yourself free to experience all of you heart and soul.

HE CAME

Our son, Lucas, was born in less than thirty days after we received that phone call. Lucas came home from the hospital with us. He entered our lives. He entered our hearts. Some people may think it happened quickly. However, the seed was planted in my heart since I was a child. The seed was planted in Pierre's heart. It was important to me. It was important to him. Thus, he came for us.

I set up Lucas's room with a blue and green comforter. A Baby Einstein mobile hung above his crib. Animal and picture frames shared shelf space. The letters L-U-C-A-S hung on the wall, along with a "Twinkle, Twinkle, Little Star" canvas.

Lucas came home from the hospital: brown hair, adorable, wide-eyed, and observant. I rocked him in the glider. He was wrapped in an onesie that revealed the wording, "I'm Loved."

Gabriel arrived home from school. I heard the patter of his footsteps. I heard his voice, "I can't wait."

The bedroom door opened. My face lit up. Pierre stood while I sat in the glider. Gabriel covered his mouth in awe. I positioned Lucas as Gabriel perched on the ottoman. I pronounced, "I'd like you to meet your brother Lucas." Gabriel tenderly held Lucas's hand. And then sweetness was uttered once again. *Gabriel listened to his heart. Gabriel listened to his soul.* "I have so much love in my heart for you." I kissed Gabriel as he expressed himself so genuinely. He shared, "I prayed and waited for you. And here you are." Pierre expressed, "He's pretty lucky to have you as his brother."

Gabriel asked me, "Do you remember when I was born?" I grinned and nodded yes. I connected, "You captured my heart the moment I laid eyes on you... Your soulful eyes penetrated deep inside me." Pierre wiped his own tears. Gabriel kissed

Lucas and enthusiastically revealed to him, "I knew you would bring light to all of us." And that is what Lucas brought... brilliance, illumination, light to the darkness.

Gabriel with his newborn brother, Lucas.

HERE YOU ARE

Gabriel shared with Lucas, "I prayed and waited for you. And here you are."

Pierre compiled a list of all the attributes he wanted in a wife. He expressed to me, "I prayed for you. And here you are."

Here they are... Gabriel and Lucas.

Like father, like son. A model of prayer... of waiting. And here you are. Wow!

Here you are. This is your life. You can dwell on the past. But the past is over. All you have is the present. You can give away your power to people, conditions, or circumstances. You can create a life of misery and pain. Or you can create a life of wonder and joy. *Here you are.* You are never too late. You are right on time... in this moment to show up better, brighter, and different—authentically you, fully present, fully engaged, and fully connected. *Here you are.* Those three words carry such amazing energy.

The Universe, Source, Spirit, God hears your prayers. Prayer opens you to commune with God. Meditation opens you to hear from God. In the stillness... in the quietness, you truly find yourself: whole, capable, balanced, aware, creative, inspiring, imaginative, and assertive. In stillness, you find yourself. Here you are.

"For what it's worth: it's never too late... to be whoever you want to be. There's no time limit, stop whenever you want. You can change or stay the same, there are no rules to this thing. We can make the best or the worst of it. I hope you make the best of it. And I hope you see things that startle you. I hope you feel things you never felt before. I hope you meet people with a different point of view. I hope you live a life you're proud of. If you find that you're not, I hope you have the courage to start all over again." ~ Eric Roth, *The Curious Case of Benjamin Button Screenplay*

Here you are!

LIFE SCRIPTS
REWRITE, REDIRECT, RECREATE

» *When have you listened to your heart?*
» *When have you listened to your soul?*
» *When was the last time you expressed yourself clearly, tenderly, genuinely?*
» *It's in you. It's in me. It's in all of us.*
» *The web of relationships. The web of interconnectedness.*
» *We came into the world to expand and express.*
» *We came into the world to love and create.*
» *We are human beings.*
» *May you feel.*
» *May you expand. May you express.*
» *May you love. May you create.*
» *May you appreciate your life!*

Sweet Illumination

Chapter 22
Loose Grip

I have learned to hold a loose grip on things now due to all the storms of my life. The tighter the clench, the more I endured and subjected myself to an unyielding approach. The looser the grip, the more I thrived and witnessed a gentler approach to life.

Many people have shared that they are too afraid to adopt. They would love to, but the "what ifs" come into play. What if you get attached and the child is taken away? What if your other children get attached and the child is taken away? There are no guarantees in life. But you must be willing to take a risk. Staying still gets you nowhere. Jumping into the wide abyss aligns you with infinite possibilities, infinite opportunities, infinite intelligence, and infinite wisdom. In other words, you get out of the way.

If Lucas was meant for us to love and raise, he's meant for us. It's our job to lead with our hearts, not our heads. Every time I led with my head, my ego got involved. EGO stands for

Erasing God Off. Every time, I led with my heart, soul, and spirit, the unimaginable resonated and flourished.

The more I let go of things, the more I receive goodness in my life. It may sound ironic. But truly, it's shifting a mindset. What would be the worst thing that could happen to you? List them. Get them off your chest. Now rip them up and breathe. You are still alive. You are still safe. You are still secure. You are still loved. You are still loving. Nothing really changed. Yes, the external things evolve. However, the internal things are always there and will always be there. Coming to the glorious awareness sets you free as you tap into the presence of your divine inner being. *When you tap into your soul, you feel the heartbeat of God and the interconnectedness of being.* That's the sweet spot where all the magic takes place and where the splendid synchronicities appear. And the best thing that occurred is you got out of the way and allowed divine inspiration to lead you.

When I lost everything in Hurricane Katrina, I could have fallen apart. My possessions could have owned me. My worth and value could have been so wrapped up in the things—the stuff. But we are not merely consumers. We are observers. And what I have observed is that the memories remain. The energy of creation remains. The love remains. It must be recognized and transformed for healing and clarity to be omnipresent in your heart and soul.

LIFE SCRIPTS
REWRITE, REDIRECT, RECREATE

» *What are you tightly holding onto?*

» *Is it the unforgiveness that crept in your heart?*

» *The little bitterness that diminished the sweetness?*

» *What are you afraid to let go of?*

» *The uncompromising relationship?*

» *The hell-bent job?*

» *The control over your teenager?*

» *The more I let go of things, the more other things come to me...*

» *The more I receive goodness in my life.*

Sweet Illumination

Chapter 23
My Garden

Are you notorious for beating yourself up? For not getting everything done on your "to do" list? Well, I can raise my hand and testify that was surely me. My inner critic beat myself up and reminded me of all the things that I didn't get to. I complained of the things that I didn't get to, and I forget to celebrate the things that I did get to.

A different mindset was required—a shifting of perspective. I shifted from guilt to compassion with a new awareness and new understanding. Guilt encompassed a feeling of remorse, whether real or imagined. Compassion allowed a feeling of sympathy, whether real or imagined. The guilt engulfed me in the imaginable. The compassion released me to the realness.

Once I delved into my subconscious mind to weed these destructive patterns from my garden, I could move forward with conscious awareness and create a lush, glorious garden. The old me lived in the realm and limits of the three ugly "C" patterns.

THE THREE UGLY "C" PATTERNS:

Criticize.

Complain.

Control.

My critical voice was a loud, incessant noise—not constructive but truly harmful. When I criticize myself, there is something I don't like about myself. When I criticize others, guess what? It really is about me again. Something I see in them is really about not liking that same part in me. It's a mirror analogy reflecting our internal world as it is projected in our outer world. The mirror of life reflects truths that are sometimes difficult to recognize and admit. But once you look into the mirror of your heart and soul, you can create a new reflection, a new reality, new understanding.

My complaining voice was an insurmountable, invincible chatter that destroyed the present moment. It evoked ungratefulness.

My controlling voice was insidious, inconspicuous, and seemly harmless. But control isn't care or unconditional love. It is "Do this because I say." It's for my benefit, not your benefit. But truthfully, it doesn't benefit either party.

So I beat myself up for not getting enough done during the day. I complained that I didn't have enough time or that the kids took up my time or that I didn't feel good. I *controlled more by doing more.* It was the exact opposite of what needed to be done. Tears cascaded. And the next day, I picked right up from where I left off... to no avail. *I was living in a survival mindset, not a thrive mindset.* And my body became my dump truck of emotions.

The sabotage patterns robbed me of pure joy. I lived with guilt. I was my own prisoner, enslaved to self-limiting beliefs, shackled to negative thoughts, stuck in the daily grind of not enjoying life.

The criticizing, complaining, controlling mindset was due to my needless suffering. Most suffering of humanity is due to the same mindset: criticizing the past, present, and bringing that same energy into the future; complaining of what you do not have instead of everything that you do have; or controlling by tightly gripping things that you ultimately have no control over.

But I do have control over my mind.

The new me had to make a choice... to deliberately create new patterns and new thoughts. It's a daily process, not a one-shot deal. But it is worth the evolution to a gentler, kinder way of life. And I discovered life-affirming patterns.

LIFE-AFFIRMING PATTERNS:

Compassion.

Gratefulness.

Celebrate.

My compassionate voice switched from guilt to compassion: compassion for myself, compassion by practicing self-care, compassion for others, and compassion for a healthier mindset. No one could give me a new mindset. I had to discover it myself. I thanked God because the universe thrilled me with unlimited possibilities.

My grateful voice became music to my ears—an intoxicating sweetness! When I wake up and before I go to bed, I give thanks. At first, I came up with listing an arbitrary number of five things that I'm grateful for. I thought it would become rote. But I was truthfully overflowing with joy because my list expounds with newness every morning and every night. My awareness has increased. I don't want to miss these moments.

I want to savor them. I've already missed too much. Now, I'm redeeming the time.

My celebratory voice enjoyed the possibilities of the day. For instance, I cooked, ran errands, bought Gabriel a new pair of shoes, cleaned Lucas's closet, walked the dog, meditated, wrote a blog, edited a screenplay, made some phone calls, answered some emails, and read a chapter of a book. Those snippets are sufficient for the day: nothing to add—nothing to delete. It was a perfect day!

What patterns do you practice? Are you aware of your sabotaging patterns? Maybe they are the three ugly "C" patterns. Maybe other patterns surface.

I encourage you to explore and discover your amazing adventure of life. You are worth so much more. May you clothe yourself in loveliness and worthiness. May you let go of the shackles of guilt and fear... the shackles of the "to do" list. May you hear the sweetness that intoxicates through the nectar of gratefulness. May you celebrate your beautiful life.

Human suffering can be put to an end when you invite a compassionate, celebratory, and grateful mindset. It's truly a choice—a shift in perspectives.

Go plant your lush, glorious garden! I can't wait to see it!

EGO VERSUS SPIRIT

Have you etched God, Spirit, and Source out? I have. More than I realized and admitted. But I desired to stay in pleasing alignment, deeply connected, and effortlessly a vibrational match to love, beauty, peace, joy, creativity, and fulfillment. I was restored, made complete, and whole. And it began with an unbounded awareness.

Ego is a false sense of "I." My ego kept me in a position that I needed to work harder. I can't make a mistake. The archetype of innocent. My strategy was to do things right. But mistakes are the evolutionary stepping stones of healing. Of beautiful and radiant light shining forth. It's the zebra. The shadow and the light blending effortlessly. Embracing it all. Owning it all.

My ego has been big, keeping me small, stuck with the same destructive patterns, thinking I knew better, believing my perceptions, taking them as truth, running in a vicious cycle. My ego did not protect me but harmed me, keeping me disconnected from Source, others, and myself.

Along my journey, *I discovered the remedy for ego is Spirit!* Spirit blossoms when all the fragments of ego melt into wholeness. There is a gentle understanding, no longer needing to figure things out. It is universal intelligence, universal wisdom, universal love, and universal oneness.

EGO...   REMEDY...   SPIRIT...

VOICE
(Our Expression)

Confuses..... *Translates*

Multiple voices..... *One voice*

Mean..... *Tender*

Critical..... *Encourager*

Yells..... *Whispers*

Attacks..... *Listens*

Blocks..... *Flows*

Unsure..... *Knowing*

Talker..... *Observer*

Lies..... *Truth*

Confusion..... *Clarity*

Imitators..... *Intuition*

Ignores..... *Recognizes*

Judges..... *Accepts*

Nitpicks..... *Beautiful*

Embellish..... *Simple*

React..... *Responds*

IDENTITY
(Our Character)

Selfish..... *Compassionate*
Broken..... *Perfect*
Incomplete..... *Complete*
Cheap..... *Priceless*
Wounded..... *Wholeness*
Stained..... *Spotless*
Victim..... *Victorious*
I'm not..... *I am*
Old..... *New*
Dead..... *Alive*
Disable..... *Able*
Stuck..... *Evolve*
Lose .... *Find*

ATTITUDE
(Our Frame of Mind)

Can't..... *Can*
Self-loathing..... *Radiant*
Hurt..... *Unharmed*
Complain..... *Grateful*
Suspicious..... *Silent*
Busy..... *Calm*
Impatient..... *Patient*
Burdensome..... *Light*

POSITION
(Our Reference Point)

Chains..... *Gifts*
Heartache..... *Treasure*
Trapped..... *Rescued*
Scars..... *Healing*
Problem..... *Opportunity*
Battle..... *Effortless*
Compete..... *Harmonious*
More..... *Sufficient*

TACTICS
(Our Patterns)

Illusions..... *Discernment*

Replays..... *Forgets*

Analyzes..... *Accepts*

Technology..... *Nature*

Excuses..... *Dreams*

Wander..... *Aims*

Counterfeit..... *Authentic*

Repels..... *Resonates*

Consume..... *Enough*

Control..... *Let go*

Tear..... *Build*

Destroy..... *Create*

Scatter..... *Master*

Unreal..... *Real*

Gorge..... *Satisfied*

Run..... *Still*

Stop..... *Go*

Hide..... *Remember*

Get..... *Give*

Withhold..... *Share*

Bury..... *Discover*

FEELING
(Our Power of Perceiving)

Anxious..... *Joy*

Fear..... *Love*

Conflict..... *Peace*

Shame..... *Glory*

Despair..... *Hope*

Gloom..... *Cheer*

Disenchanted..... *Amazed*

Contract..... *Expand*

STATE
(Our Capacity)

Boundaries..... *Boundless*
Limited..... *Eternal*
Tick-tock..... *Timeless*
Closed..... *Open*
Struggles..... *Effortless*
Trivial..... *Purposeful*
Me-ness..... *Oneness*
Blind..... *Aware*
Mind..... *Heart*
Body..... *Soul*
Sickness..... *Health*
Bondage..... *Freedom*
Force..... *Power*
Miry pit..... *Presence*
Having..... *Being*
Blame..... *Surrender*
Defend..... *Reasonable*
Traps..... *Rhythm*
Distant..... *Connection*
Numb..... *Pulsating*
Petrifies..... *Vibrates*
Discord..... *Unity*
Discriminates..... *Brotherhood*
Robot (Autopilot)..... *Conscious*

CONDITION
(How Things Go)

Conditional.....	*Unconditional*
Impossible.....	*Possible*
Changes.....	*Constant*
Uncertainty.....	*Certainty*
Wrong-mind.....	*Right-mind*
Danger.....	*Safe*
Expose.....	*Clothe*
Scarcity.....	*Abundant*
Weak.....	*Strength*
Dark.....	*Light*
Doubt.....	*Faith*
Projects.....	*Extends*
Worry.....	*Trust*
Asleep.....	*Awake*
Thinking.....	*Sensing*
Believing.....	*Experiencing*
Repeat.....	*Undo*
Follow.....	*Lead*
Scatter.....	*Belong*

You can't get around ego. You have to go through every crevice and facet to discover the radiance of Spirit.

May your peace be restored. And may you realize that you are powerful beyond measure once you tap in, tune in, and turn in... to the frequency of Spirit, Energy, and Source. It's a field of unlimited potential and unlimited possibilities. You just have to let go of that tight grip of the ego. Pluck it from you hand to embrace the hand of love and peace. How do I know? I lived it. I experienced it. And I released it.

I am no longer *Erasing God Off* (EGO). I'm paying attention to destructive patterns of thoughts and behaviors. I am aligned and connected through meditation and mindfulness. My ultimate healing and divine clarity occurs through my writing.

Writing helps the messages sink deeper into every unturned crevice of my protective ego. I've learned that I'm every character that I write about, unearthing truths of me—embodying all of me.

Let go of control and welcome the manifestation of the glory of God. The remedy for ego is indeed Spirit!

Sweet Illumination

Chapter 24
Crashing Waves

As I gently observed the calm of the rhythmic waves, I experienced the raging waves in my moods, thoughts, and emotions. I longed for the steadfast calm, the belaboring balance, the harvest of harmony. Yet, I found peace, not by avoiding the raging waters, but by entering them and the fire within me. **LIFE STORMS** is a story about endurance, faith, love, peace. The storms of life crash upon us momentarily... until we rise again triumphantly.

A song, "You Make Me Brave" by Amanda Cook, played.

> *As Your love, in wave after wave*
> *Crashes over me, crashes over me*
> *You make me brave*
> *You make me brave*
>
> *You call me out beyond the shore into the waves*
> *You make me brave*
> *You make me brave*
>
> *No fear can hinder now the love that a made a way*

We headed to Moonlight State Beach in Encinitas. Pierre and Lucas built sand castles. Gabriel collected shells in a bucket.

I penned in my journal:

"A search for normal, a quest for perfection, a quietness in my soul. Comparing, analyzing, wrestling, over-thinking the 'what ifs.'"

Gabriel viewed my sorrowful expression. He selected a piece of blue-green sea glass from the bucket. Gabriel flattered, "Like your beautiful eyes. Your eyes are very blue green like the ocean." I admired his simple token.

Meanwhile, Pierre and Lucas rinsed their hands in the ocean. Gabriel dropped the bucket and dashed in the water to wet his feet.

I wrote, "As I awake and undo, I truly discover myself and accept what is, no longer stuck in what could have been."

Robert Louis Stevenson advised, *"Keep your eyes open to your mercies. The man who forgets to be thankful has fallen asleep."* I don't want to be asleep anymore, not just at the wheel, but in life in general. I want to be wide awake, wide open—a wide receiver.

Gabriel yelled, "Come on Mom." I freely proceeded into the water.

It is what is. Perfect. I let go, drop the barriers, and return to love... return to joy.

Gabriel offered, "It's cold." I elaborated, "Brr. Brr. Freezing!" Pierre smiled.

Lucas gleefully fell with his weighed-down pants. I rolled his pants up. With a mischievous face, Lucas teased, "Bet you can't catch me!" I chased after him.

Jennifer entered the Pacific Ocean with Gabriel and Lucas.

Gabriel and Lucas exited the cold water.

A song, such as "Wake Me Up" by Aloe Blacc played.

Feeling my way through the darkness
Guided by a beating heart

I can't tell where the journey will end
But I know where to start
They tell me I'm too young to understand
They say I'm caught up in a dream
Well life will pass me by if I don't open up my eyes
Well that's fine by me

So wake me up when it's all over
When I'm wiser and I'm older
All this time I was finding myself, and I
Didn't know I was lost
I didn't know I was lost
I didn't know I was lost
I didn't know I was lost
I didn't know

NOTHING TO FIX

My mantra for the day was *"Go fix Jennifer."* It was a chant that played in my head. Do more. Figure it out. But this mantra left me depleted and exhausted.

The simple truth: *There is nothing to fix. There is nothing broken.* Breathe that in because it's powerful. *It's a shift from fixing to finding.* I had to find myself... my authentic self: my voice, my heart, my soul. I was lost in my thoughts. My head was leading me not to lie down in green pastures but to live in survival mode: a fight or flight state of mind... a fight or flight state of being. Dangerous indeed.

There is nothing to fix. There is only the journey of finding yourself, discovering who you are, and exploring the deep chambers of your heart and soul.

What I realized is... there really is no self-improvement. You are not a project to fix. You are not a project to endure. You are not a to-do list item to check off. You are not broken. You are whole. You are perfect. You are powerful beyond measure.

What I found was my self-worth, self-love, self-care, self-awareness, self-validation, self-forgiveness, self-compassion, and self-empowerment. I'm changing the definition of *self-improvement* to *self-empowerment.* The connotation is slight, gentle, and powerful. I've been on a self-empowering journey. I have abandoned myself for too long.

You discover one of the most important relationships... a relationship with yourself! You are the one you have been waiting for. It's a powerful relationship that God waits patiently for us to discover. He equips, He sustains, and He protects. He is your shield and your comforter. *The more we are empowered, the more the divine qualities manifest.* The more we can hear the voice of God, the more we can be in sync with His heart, see His vision, experience His healing, and witness His clarity.

Mantra of the day: *"Go find yourself."* It's a sacred journey full of spiritual and psychological growth and expansive experiences of love and joy. Let go. Push off. Keep your eyes open and celebrate.

You are the one you have been waiting for. You are magnificent, whole, perfect, and capable. Find yourself. Find your self-empowerment. Find your heart and soul.

You are not wanted. You are needed. Everyone has a part to sing in the choir.

LIFE SCRIPTS
REWRITE, REDIRECT, RECREATE

» *What are your passions?*

» *What makes you smile? What gets you excited?*

» *What makes you unique?*

» *What contribution did you come to bring to the world?*

» *You are not wanted. You are needed.*
  Everyone has a part to sing in the choir.

Sweet Illumination

Chapter 25
Aftermath Of Hurricane Katrina

On August 29, 2005, Hurricane Katrina blew into the Gulf of Mexico, wreaking havoc on the Gulf Coast and Louisiana. Our roof blew off and rainwater spilled into the house. Furthermore, the levees broke, and floodwater filled the house.

We evacuated on August 28th to Baton Rouge, Louisiana, and Houston, Texas for three weeks. We moved thirteen times before we called Encinitas, California home. We always wanted to move to California. However, we didn't think the universe would answer through the means of a hurricane.

As Hurricane Rita blew into Texas, a family posted housing in San Diego. We responded to the email that we'd take the apartment for one year. I offered, "God's will be done" as I hit "enter." In that moment, the lights went out. We lost power once again. Welcome hurricane!

I learned big lessons about myself, others, what I valued, and life itself.

"Put your ear down close to your soul and listen hard." ~ Anne Saxon. I had to listen to what really mattered.

LESSONS FROM HURRICANE KATRINA

~ We are alive. Isn't that beautiful in itself? Naked we come into the world. Naked we return.

~ We have everything we need. I realized that I had a gorgeous home filled with beautiful things. But once it was taken away, those things didn't own me. They never did. They were just tools to be used and enjoyed and a home to open and extend fellowship.

~ There are amazing people in this world full of love and compassion in their hearts. We are thankful for the Huffmans entering our life full of zeal when we had nothing to give. They called their friends together, set up an apartment within a week, and furnished it with things that made us feel at home. Gabriel was three-years-old at the time. He awoke to his new bedroom filled with the wonder of Mickey Mouse® and Buzz Lightyear! And we delighted in a friendship that has carried through the years!

~ The world is safe, kind, and loving. I am safe, secure, loved, and loving.

~ Change is inevitable. Change is certain. Go with the flow, the seasons of life, the unexpected.

~ When Pierre and I dated, we knew that we would adopt one day. It took us being positioned in San Diego to receive Lucas. Who would have thought that Hurricane Katrina brought the beauty of a child into our hearts and our home?

~ Gabriel was scheduled for his 11th surgery two months after Hurricane Katrina. The doctor showed compassion and changed the surgical plan. Dr. Bauer did not insert tissue expanders. Instead, Gabriel underwent serial incisions. A three-month break of not filling tissue expanders was extraordinary when we had other pieces of our life to rebuild.

~ Three months after Hurricane Katrina, we received an offer on our destroyed home on Thanksgiving Day, and we accepted.

Much to be thankful for! Lessons, opportunities, growth... this encompasses all experiences: the amazing journey and celebration of life.

LIFE SCRIPTS
REWRITE, REDIRECT, RECREATE

» *What are you thankful for?*
» *What lessons did you learn, grow, and expand the most?*
» *What lessons were repeated and took you the longest to understand?*
» *Who are your greatest teachers?*

A DETOUR

We drove back to Louisiana in the same green SUV with a U-Haul® hitch. I gazed out of the window. As I embraced the uncertainty, I found inner peace and needed rest for my soul. Signage revealed, "Welcome to Louisiana." Pierre grabbed my knee. He consoled, "A different season. That's all." I smiled and reflected calmness.

ANOTHER HURRICANE

We resided in Chenier Apartments in Mandeville, Louisiana for a year. The inside décor resembled California with the sweet family photos at Moonlight State Beach, shabby chic couch, seashells and succulent knickknacks resided on a driftwood table. However, the big windows with transoms and open blinds reflected the outside gloom and another life storm.

Hurricane Isaac (2012) visited the coast of Louisiana seven years to the day of Hurricane Katrina. Torrential rain ensued.[24]

Pierre, Gabriel, Lucas, and I convened around our round kitchen table. Chicken parmesan and Caesar salad filled their blue plates.

Lucas shared, "My teacher taught us the hurricane categories." Gabriel added, "Bet you didn't know those in California?! Here, you better know them." Lucas counted on his hand. "They go from 1, 2, 3, 4. And 5 isn't good!"

The lights flickered. Lucas flinched and lowered his head. I rubbed Lucas. I elaborated, "I get scared sometimes too."

Gabriel asked, "Was Hurricane Katrina a Category 5? Pierre explained, "It was until it made landfall as a Category 3." Gabriel exasperated, "And this season visits us yearly!" He nodded his head in disbelief. Pierre claimed, "It's what we know and how we live." Gabriel explored, "People think we're crazy for coming back."

Lucas asked, "Was I in Hurricane Katrina?" Gabriel touched Lucas's shoulder. Gabriel said, "You were born in California. Probably why you can pee in the ocean." Gabriel pointed to himself. "I was born in the south. Explains why I can't pee in the ocean."

Pierre affirmed, "But you can survive a hurricane!"

I gave Pierre a look: "Are you sure about this?" Pierre declared, "We're staying."

The wind howled. The lights went out. The boys screamed.

Lucas spoke, "I'm scared!" I reassured, "You're safe." Gabriel explored, "What do we do now?" Pierre disclosed,

"Ride it out." Gabriel responded, "Pray and hope power comes on."

A transformer blew. The abrupt wind opened the front door. Gabriel remarked, "A tornado!" Lucas mentioned, "Wish we were in California."

Pierre observed the terror in his boys and grabbed his car keys. Pierre pronounced, "Hell with this. Let's go!"

A Switchfoot song, such as "Hello Hurricane," played.

> *Hello hurricane, you're not enough*
> *Hello hurricane, you can't silence my love*
> *I've got doors and windows boarded up*
> *All your dead end fury is not enough*
> *You can't silence my love, yeah my love*
>
> *I'm a fighter fighting for control*
> *I'm a fighter fighting for my soul*
> *Everything inside of me surrenders*
> *You can't silence my love*
> *You can't silence my love, yeah*

WHERE WE ARE NOW

I published my first book under the series *Life Storms*. There will be more to come. Stay tuned.

Our home was for sale for four years in California. We went back to Louisiana for three of those years, but we returned to California once again and called it home. Now, we are thriving!

Pierre and I have been married for twenty years now.

Gabriel, 13, has undergone 13 major surgeries and two laser procedures. He wants to be a doctor, video game developer, and inventor.

Lucas, 8, wants to be a football player, race car driver, and hockey player.

Please visit www.nevus.org for more information on Giant Pigmented Nevus or consider a donation. Giant Pigmented Nevus occurs in 1 in 500,000 births. Neurocutaneous melanosis occurs in 1 in a million. There are approximately 860 children and 375 adults with Giant Pigmented Nevus. There is no known cure—*yet*.

There are millions of children worldwide, including the U.S., waiting to be adopted. Will you please consider opening your heart to expansive love?

Hurricane Katrina was the deadliest and most destructive Atlantic hurricane of the 2005 Atlantic season. There were 1,893 confirmed fatalities. Katrina formed on August 23, 2005 and dissipated on August 30, 2005. Areas affected included Bahamas, South Florida, Cuba, Louisiana (especially Greater New Orleans), Mississippi, Alabama, Florida Panhandle, and most of eastern North America.

CREDITS ROLL.
FADE TO BLACK.

LIFE SCRIPTS
REWRITE, REDIRECT, RECREATE

» *Are you prepared for another Life Storm?*
» *Everyone has a Life Script.*
» *Who wrote your Life Script?*
» *Did you follow it, accept it, or change it?*
» *May you revise your Life Script with intention and awareness.*
» *May you have the courage to start over.*
» *Now is the perfect time to tune into your life.*
» *How does your Life Script end?*

Life Storms: Hurricane Katrina
Notes

LIFE SCRIPTS 1 – THE CATALYST

1. **Nevus Outreach, Inc.**
   http://www.nevus.org/

2. **Natural Disasters - International Federation of Red Cross and Red Crescent Societies**
   http://www.ifrc.org/en/what-we-do/disaster-management/about-disasters/what-is-a-disaster/

3. **10 World Worst Disasters - Disasterium Natural & Man Made Disasters**
   http://www.disasterium.com/10-worst-natural-disastersof-all-time/

4. **10 US Worst Disasters - LiveScience**
   http://www.livescience.com/11365-10-worst-natural-disasters.html

5. **Hurricane Research Division - Atlantic Oceanographic and Meteorological Laboratory**
   http://www.aoml.noaa.gov/index.html

6. **National Weather Service National Hurricane Service - Saffir-Simpson Hurricane Wind Scale**
   http://www.nhc.noaa.gov/aboutsshws.php

7. **The New Orleans Hurricane of 1915 - From Wikipedia, the free encyclopedia**
   http://en.wikipedia.org/wiki/1915_New_Orleans_hurricane

8. **The Louisiana Hurricane of 1940 - From Wikipedia, the free encyclopedia**
   http://en.wikipedia.org/wiki/1940_Louisiana_hurricane

9. Major Hurricane of 1947 - From Wikipedia, the free encyclopedia

http://en.wikipedia.org/wiki/1947_Fort_Lauderdale_hurricane
http://old-new-orleans.com/NO_1947_hurricane

10. Hurricane Betsy (1965) - From Wikipedia, the free encyclopedia

http://en.wikipedia.org/wiki/Hurricane_Betsy

11. Hurricane Camille (1969) - NOAA/ National Weather Service National Centers for Environmental Prediction National Hurricane Center

http://www.nhc.noaa.gov/outreach/history/

12. Hurricane Katrina (2005) - NOAA/ National Weather Service National Centers for Environmental Prediction National Hurricane Center

http://www.nhc.noaa.gov/outreach/history/

13. Hurricane Katrina (2005) - From Wikipedia, the free encyclopedia

http://en.wikipedia.org/wiki/Hurricane_Katrina

14. Okeechobee Hurricane (1928) - From Wikipedia, the free encyclopedia

http://en.wikipedia.org/wiki/1928_Okeechobee_hurricane

15. Hurricane Wilma (2005) - NOAA/ National Weather Service National Centers for Environmental Prediction National Hurricane Center

http://www.nhc.noaa.gov/outreach/history/

16. Hurricane Rita (2005) - NOAA/ National Weather Service National Centers for Environmental Prediction National Hurricane Center

http://www.nhc.noaa.gov/outreach/history/

17. Hurricane Ophelia (2005) - NOAA/ National Weather Service National Centers for Environmental Prediction National Hurricane Center

http://www.nhc.noaa.gov/outreach/history/

18. Hurricane Dennis (2005) - NOAA/ National Weather Service National Centers for Environmental Prediction National Hurricane Center

http://www.nhc.noaa.gov/outreach/history/

LIFE SCRIPTS 2 – THE EVACUATION

19. **Hurricane Katrina (2005)**
    http://en.wikipedia.org/wiki/Hurricane_Katrina
    http://en.wikipedia.org/wiki/
    Effects_of_Hurricane_Katrina_in_New_Orleans

20. **Hurricane Rita (2005) - NOAA National Oceanic and Atmospheric Administration**
    http://www.stormsurge.noaa.gov/event_history_ 2000s.html

LIFE SCRIPTS 3 – COMING HOME

21. **17th Street Canal - From Wikipedia, the free encyclopedia**
    http://en.wikipedia.org/wiki/17th_Street_Canal

22. **New Orleans Bomb Shelter**
    http://noadventure.com/bomb-shelter/

23. **New Orleans Bomb Shelter**
    https://answers.yahoo.com/questions/index

LIFE SCRIPTS 5 – SWEET ILLUMINATION

24. **Hurricane Isaac (2012) - From Wikipedia, the free encyclopedia**
    http://en.wikipedia.org/wiki/Hurricane_Isaac_%282012%29

Life Storms: Hurricane Katrina
Music Copyrights

"Only Love" by Ben Howard

Written by Ben Howard
© 2011 WARNER/CHAPPELL MUSIC PUBLISHING LTD
All Rights Reserved.

"Come Home" by One Republic

Written by Ryan Tedder
© Sony/ATV Tunes LLC, Midnite Miracle Music, Universal Music Publishing Ltd., Sony/ATV Harmony Uk, Velvet Hammer Music
All Rights Reserved. Used by Permission.

"Beautiful Things" by Gungor

Written by Lisa Gungor and Michael Gungor
© 2009 worshiptogether.com Songs (ASCAP) (administered at CapitolCMG Publishing.com). All rights reserved. Used by permission.

"You Make Me Brave" by Bethel Music and Amanda Cook

Written by Amanda Cook
© 2013 Bethel Music Publishing (ASCAP). All Rights Reserved. Used by Permission.

"Wake Me Up" by Aloe Blacc

Words and Music by Aloe Blacc, Tim Bergling and Michael Einziger
© 2013 WB Music Corp. (ASCAP), Aloe Blacc Publishing (ASCAP), EMI
Music Publishing Scandinavia AB (STIM) and Elementary Particle Music (ASCAP)
All Rights on Behalf of Itself and Aloe Blacc Publishing Administered by WB Music Corp.
All Rights Reserved. Used by Permission.

"Hello Hurricane" by Switchfoot

Written by Jon Foreman and Tim Foreman
Publishing Schmublishing Publishing © 2009
All Rights Reserved. Used by Permission.

*All music licenses have been obtained. Please forgive any omissions in exact wording.

About the Author

Jennifer Gremillion is a screenwriter, blogger, and *Life Scripts* author. As a survivor of many storms in life, *Life Storms: Hurricane Katrina* is her first installment of the *Life Storms* series. *Life Scripts* are written by others and handed to us. Most people are actors following scripts given to them. Some people don't question and don't change it. But there are others who discard it and edit their own script. Jennifer Gremillion chose the latter: to edit, direct, and create her own *Life Script.*

She became the master of her heart and soul and tossed out all other scripts. Her evolving screenplays include **LIFE STORMS, NEW YEAR'S RESOLUTION, UNFORESEEN,** and **SAM CARES.** Jennifer Gremillion holds a M.A. Along her journey, she discovered her love of writing as a teenager when she wrote an essay, *How to Describe the Color Red to a Blind Person,* and penned *Who Am I? Why Am I Here? What Is My Purpose?* Her internal healing has greatly contributed to her writing. Every life experience has been a teacher, lover, and healer. Her inspirational blog posts can be enjoyed on her website: www.jennifergremillion.com. Jennifer Gremillion resides in Southern California with her husband, two sons, and dog.

CPSIA information can be obtained at www.ICGtesting.com
Printed in the USA
LVOW02s0710110815

449574LV00002B/2/P